THE ULTIMATE GUIDE TO
B2B
SALES
PROSPECTING

4 steps to unlock your hidden market

RICHARD FORREST

"We have been working together and using Richard's team for 5 years and I would say that about half of my clients have come from the sales leads generated by Richard's approach and team."

Greg Puttick – General Manager – EL Blue

"I would definitely recommend Richard's approach. The quality of clients we have been able to bring on board through the work of Richard and his team has probably paid for their services for the next 20 years."

Bill Alexiou-Hucker – Director – GPSM

"The approach that Richard's team have taken has been absolutely fantastic. They have understood our business, what we want to achieve from lead generation, and then made it happen. The fact that they have the right people in their business in the right roles and that their prospecting process works so well just makes it fantastic from our perspective."

Josh Sanders – General Manager (NSW Industrial) – GraysOnline

"The number of new sales meetings we have been able to go to is really beyond my expectations and we are now converting these into sales."

Andrew Mansfield – Director Client Solutions – Genesis Instore Marketing

"For any business focused on growth, sales prospecting is a strategy worth exploring and may well be the right option for your company. Using the process recommended by Richard allows our Agents to meet with well-qualified prospects. They can concentrate their efforts on what they do best, and that's speaking with people face-to-face about their insurance needs, assessing what they have in place and determining if there is a better, more effective solution required to ensure the right protection is in place."

Anne Lucas, National Manager – Marketing & Communications, Elders Insurance

"As a sales manager of a highly established company one of the most difficult tasks for a sales team is continually finding new sales leads. When first approached by FMG to discuss sales lead generation I believed it was something we could do internally, however after going to see FMG head office and seeing what they do and how they do it, I decided to throw the idea around our business. After discussions we decided to move ahead with Richard's system, thinking that for a small investment it was worth the risk. I was amazed to listen in and find that the team making the calls sounded like they could be from my company, they were highly persuasive but without being pushy, appointments were made then and there. From the leads generated using this approach, the close ratio is very high, above 90% close on all appointments made. With Richard's strategy on how to approach the market, success is almost certainly guaranteed."

Andrew Meadows, Territory Sales Manager – TNT Express

First published in 2017 by Richard Forrest

First Edition

© Richard Forrest 2017
The moral rights of the author have been asserted

National Library of Australia Cataloguing-in-Publication entry:
   Creator: Forrest, Richard, author.
   Title: The ultimate guide to B2B sales prospecting.
   ISBN: 9781925648355 (paperback)
   Subjects: Internet marketing – Handbooks, manuals, etc.
               Electronic commerce.
               Entrepreneurship.
               Success in business.

Editing + Proofreading by Cavalletti Communications, www.cavacom.biz
Cover design by Peter Reardon
Project management and text design by Michael Hanrahan Publishing

CONTENTS

CONTENTS

INTRODUCTION

The Internet has inalterably changed the world of sales. So much of the grunt work that used to be done by salespeople is now done by digital marketing campaigns, or often even by the customer. This is particularly true in the world of B2B sales, where buyers often come to the table knowing almost as much about our products or services as we do.

In the rush to move with the customer into email inboxes and onto social media platforms, we have lost sight of something important. We have forgotten what all salespeople once took for granted: that sales depend on our ability to reach out to customers and engage them in conversation. The conversation is the beating heart at the centre of the sale. This conversation is personal, reciprocal, and relational. Digital marketing is rarely any of these things. Instead of searching for new customers, we are relying far too much on digital marketing to put feelers out for us. This means we are allowing our customers to determine how, when and if they approach us. We are allowing them to start the conversation with us and to determine its content. This isn't really the selling game so much as the waiting game.

We've accepted this as the new sales paradigm, and why wouldn't we? Digital marketing produces a steady enough trickle of sales leads, and following up on those leads is much easier than finding a new prospect and starting a conversation with them from scratch. If we are hitting (or nearly hitting) our sales targets, we're happy enough to stick with the status quo. If we're not hitting our targets, we work to refine our marketing materials or to otherwise hone our approach to generating leads online. If this still isn't enough, we are far too willing to just shrug our shoulders and say, "C'est la vie."

But what if we've accepted this paradigm without first interrogating it? What if we are taking as given something that's anything but? What if we're letting slip through our fingers the chance not only to meet our sales targets but to blow them out of the water? What if there is an untapped but rich vein of prospects out there, one that is just out of sight? I'm here to tell you that there *is* an undiscovered mother lode, a wealth of opportunities lying right beneath our feet. We just need to start looking and then start digging.

But why have we stopped looking? Because we've forgotten what every salesperson once knew: that sales are the result of a created or discovered need. To find customers who need what we are selling, we need to go to them. It's not enough simply to wait for them to come to us. For those prospects who know they have a need and are already looking for what we are selling, digital marketing is doing a fine job of getting them to notice us and, if it is done right, it is helping us stand out from our competitors. But for those prospects who aren't yet looking for what we are selling, those who have not yet realised that their current situation can be solved or improved, digital marketing isn't enough. We need to tap these prospects on the shoulder and get them to see us (perhaps for the first time). To do this, we need to change our sales paradigm.

We need to start thinking about our potential markets in a new way. Think of your market like an iceberg. At the moment, most of your sales efforts are being directed at the part of the iceberg that is floating on top of the water. This is the tip of the iceberg, and this is the market you're currently addressing with your digital marketing campaigns. These are the prospects who are looking for what you sell, probably online. They are in the process of comparing you with your competitors. This is only a small portion of your potential market, though. The rest of your iceberg (a full 80% of your potential market) sits unseen below the waterline. It is made of the prospects you are currently ignoring. They aren't looking for you, and if you're like most companies, your sales team isn't really looking for them.

This book is all about how to get below the waterline. It is about how to first identify and then to engage with this broader market. As the Founder and Managing Director of Forrest Marketing Group, one of Australia's top Business-to-Business (B2B) business development agencies, I have built my business around doing just this. My team and I have been prospecting beneath the waterline, exposing the hidden parts of our clients' icebergs. Day after day and year after year, we've generated qualified sales leads for our clients.

We work for some of Australia's largest and best-known companies, and we've worked for countless SMEs as well. Whether large or small, our clients quickly learn that we deliver on our promise to produce a steady stream of qualified leads. In the last decade, we have made over four million calls, generating hundreds of thousands of qualified sales leads for our clients. These leads have turned into hundreds of millions of dollars in sales revenue. When we first made contact, the majority of these leads weren't actively looking for what our clients were selling. They were submerged beneath the waterline, but we have brought them to the surface, making them visible to our clients' sales teams, helping them make sales that they didn't even know were out there.

The secret to our success is simple: we've prospected in what might be called "the old-fashioned way". We are cold calling—engaging decision makers in person-to-person conversation. Through these conversations, we are introducing these prospects to our clients. Are our calls perceived as cold calls? Absolutely not. They're sales discovery calls, and they are uncovering issues and showing decision makers how our clients can provide appropriate solutions.

The approach we take is imitable, able to produce results for anybody who applies it diligently and consistently. It's the key that unlocks hidden local and national markets, revealing a business's true potential and then helping reach that potential. By using the strategy outlined in these pages, you'll be adding new hot prospects to your sales pipeline every day. You'll be engaging them in business-winning conversations and generating a steady stream of new sales.

My focus has always been on B2B sales, so this book takes it for granted that you, too, are in the B2B game. Many of the issues, principles, and strategies we'll discuss in what follows are appropriate for both B2B and B2C (Business-to-Consumer) sales, but where the two markets diverge, so too will their sales strategies. Provided you are in the B2B arena, the strategies in this book will prove effective, no matter how complex your product or service.

There are countless books on the market that tell you how to sell. However, very few books talk about how to use P2P (person-to-person) prospecting as an effective twenty-first-century sales strategy, and an even smaller number explain how to find the prospects you need to be talking to. Without knowing whom to call, no amount of sales strategy will do you any good. This is why the second section of this book provides detailed guidance on how to identify and define your target market, as well as what to say to them when you reach out and make contact. Following my advice will mean that you'll be looking at your iceberg below the waterline, and you'll be amazed just how large this submerged part of your market is. Your website and marketing efforts might be reaching some of these people, but the vast majority of them are—at least for now—unaware of your organisation and what it can do for them. Whether you are a salesperson looking for strategies to improve your results and get ahead of your peers, or a sales manager looking for ways to make your sales team more effective, this book will show you how to do that.

In this book, you will learn how to shine a light on a huge but untapped potential market, one that your competitors are probably ignoring. You'll learn how to broaden your focus so you're looking at your entire market rather than just the tip of the iceberg. You'll also learn how to approach these new potential customers in the right way—in a way that will ensure you are front of mind whenever they are ready to purchase, whether that is now or in two years' time. You'll learn how to start and maintain that all-important conversation that your competitors almost certainly aren't having with these prospects. My strategy is founded on the power of conversation. It takes as its starting point a two-way dialogue between your sales team and their prospects. This person-to-person conversation is exactly what has been, in effect, thrown out with the bathwater in the rush to capitalise on undeniably powerful Digital-Age marketing tools and methods. It's time to revive it.

In the final part of this book, I've provided my four-step method for effective person-to-person (P2P) prospecting. Today's prospects need to be approached in very specific ways to be turned into customers, and the four steps that we'll cover later will enable you to do this. You'll learn how to engage prospects in conversations and how to turn those conversations into opportunities. You will improve your bottom line almost immediately, but there's more. The true impact of diligent and proactive P2P prospecting will be a business that is prepared for the road ahead. You'll be turning that trickle in your pipeline into a smoothly flowing current that will continue to deliver qualified sales leads and sales day after day, month and month, and year after year.

Let's begin.

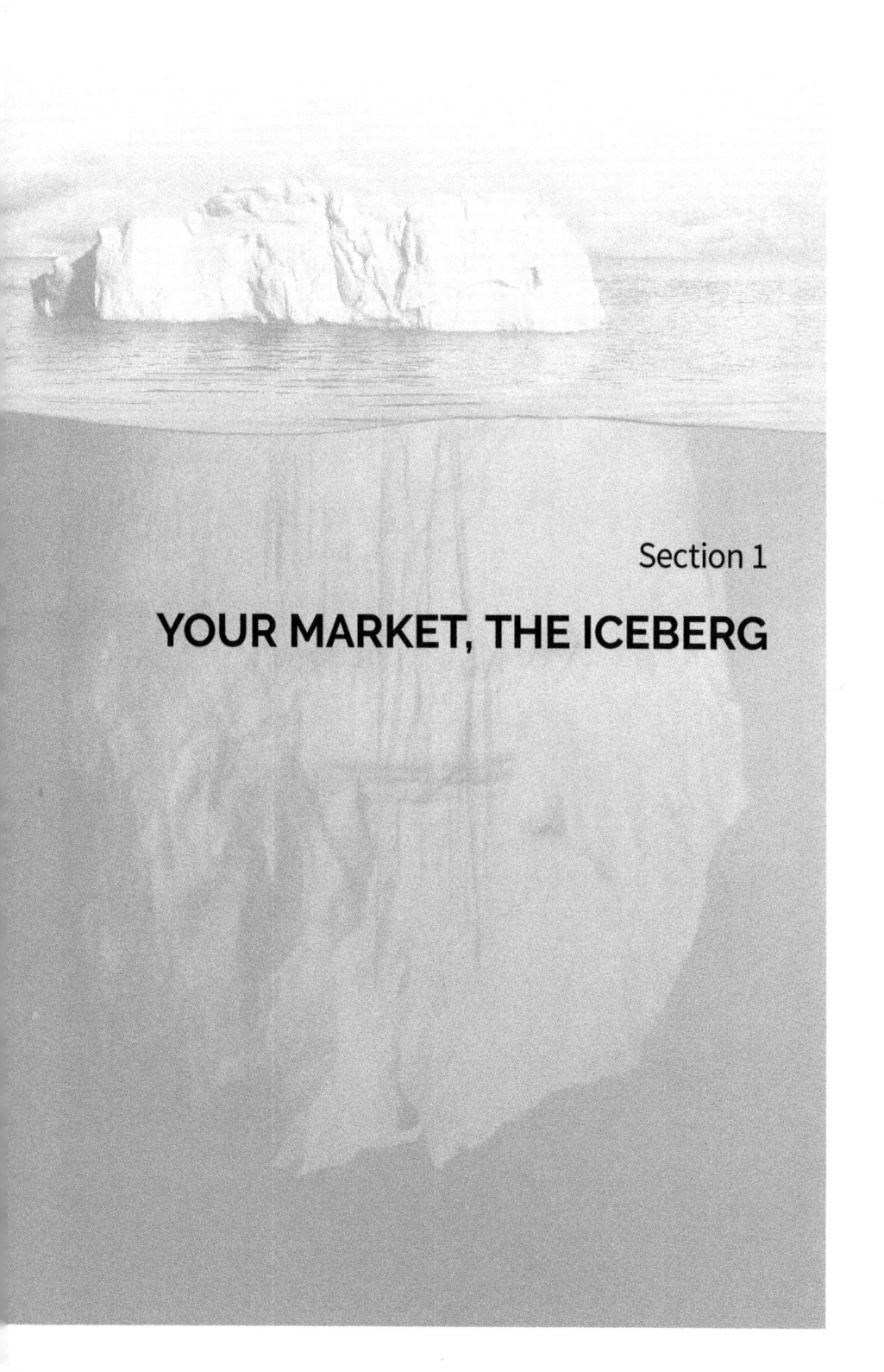

Section 1

YOUR MARKET, THE ICEBERG

Chapter 1
THE TIP OF THE ICEBERG

BEFORE the Internet dramatically changed the sales landscape, P2P prospecting was a way of life. It was something almost every salesperson *had* to learn how to do. In only a handful of industries could a salesperson make do without it. Effective prospecting is what set the sales stars apart from their underperforming peers. Effective P2P prospecting was what helped organisations build robust pipelines of sales opportunities, which meant sales today, tomorrow, and, if the pipeline was *really* robust, sales for the rest of the year.

Automated marketing has made us complacent. Companies might believe that they have a great sales pipeline that is chock-full of digitally nurtured prospects. What they actually have, though, is an out-of-date database of people. They know next to nothing about these prospects' evolving needs, and it is highly likely that next to none of their e-marketing messages are being opened (let alone read). Spam cannons (long the first resort of marketing departments) have killed the effectiveness of e-marketing.

In a recent article, Tamara Schenk (the Research Director of CSO Insights) said that, year after year, the biggest inhibitor to sales success has been our inability to communicate value messages. Why is this? It is a result of the diminishing effectiveness of e-marketing. More and more messages are being delivered to prospects who don't open them. We're not engaging with our prospects, and they are growing tired of this one-way communication street. Ask yourself this: when was the last time you responded to a marketing email, even if you were slightly interested in the solution? The chances are that your answer will be "a long time ago". We need a new (or perhaps old) way to approach the prospects in our pipeline.

In the past, a robust pipeline meant not just focusing on having a steady stream of hot prospects to sell to today. It was about building and maintaining relationships with a large number of sales prospects who were in the various stages of the sales cycle. Some were not yet ready to buy, others were kicking tyres, still others were on the cusp of a purchase. We built relationships through two-way conversations with prospects, not just on one-way automated marketing messages.

Robust pipelines were (and still are) the product of a long-term view of selling, which means accepting that not everyone is going to buy today; some will buy tomorrow, and some will buy next year, but the successful approach to prospecting was built on the view that all qualified prospects would purchase at some time or another—it was just a matter of whether they would purchase from you or from your competitors. Having a robust pipeline wasn't a set-it-and-forget-it operation. It meant building relationships with prospects every day so that when they were ready to buy, you would be their first port of call. It meant salespeople having conversations with their prospects, not passing off to marketing those prospects who weren't immediately ready to buy.

Developing and maintaining a robust pipeline meant constantly feeding new prospects into the pipe. No matter how good they were, no salesperson closed 100% of their opportunities. Usually, it was around 10-20%, so for every sale that the prospector won they would add another five to 10 new prospects to their pipeline. Failure to do this meant a pipeline that would slowly dwindle down to nothing, and as went the pipeline, so went the sales numbers.

Success in prospecting came down to two variables: quantity and quality. Quantity refers to the number of qualified prospects you are talking to and feeding into your pipeline; quality does not refer to the quality of the prospects but, rather, your ability to sell them. Without quality in your sales process, you can have all the qualified leads in the world, but you'll never be able to land enough of them to meet your targets. Without quantity, you can be the best salesperson in the world, but you aren't going to be talking to enough prospects to hit your quotas. The prospector who found the right balance of quantity and quality would win sales consistently, week after week, year after year. It was a formula that worked for generations. New salespeople would join the team, be shown the ropes, and, often on their first day, they'd be calling new prospects.

Of course, salespeople didn't source all of their own leads. The company's marketing programmes provided a reasonably steady supply of leads for the sales team to sell to, but few salespeople relied entirely upon these leads. Forward-thinking salespeople supplemented these leads by generating leads of their own. By feeding their own pipelines, they could ensure that they would hit their sales targets. They would do this by networking, attending exhibitions, researching the market and calling to introduce themselves to companies who might be able to use their products or services. Failure to do this would invariably catch up with them in the form of missed targets and, eventually, an inglorious exit from the company.

CROWDED TRAPS

This all changed with the introduction of the Internet and particularly with the growth of online marketing as a sales tool. These developments have, by and large, turned us into lazy salespeople. We have abandoned the difficult work of sales prospecting in favour of much easier but less effective ways of selling. The moment online marketing started producing a steadier stream of prospects, we grew dependent on these leads. We started expecting online marketing to live up to its proponents' many promises—namely, that online marketing would deliver us better prospects, more prospects, or even sales themselves. We've forgotten that to produce great sales results we still need to prospect (and prospect proactively) every single day. Two traps have lulled us into a false sense of security:

- **Trap 1 – Online marketing can deliver to Sales all the prospects it needs.**

  This is one of the promises online marketing advocates make, and we seem to have taken them entirely at their word, believing that online marketing (and online marketing alone) will deliver enough leads to meet the sales team's day-to-day needs. We believe that with e-mails, e-newsletters, online advertising and social media we can e-prospect and e-nurture our way to consistently great sales. This trap is incredibly seductive. After all, we can find almost anything we want online with a few mouse clicks, and anybody who is looking for what we're selling can do the same. They simply look us up online and contact us when they are ready to purchase. All we need to do is have a team of sales people standing by, waiting for the customer calls or emails to come. Stagnating or dwindling sales results show that it just isn't that easy.

- **Trap 2 – By the time we reach them (or they reach us), customers have already decided who they want to buy from.**

  Our customers are better educated about what they purchase than ever before. They often do extensive research online, which means that, when a customer contacts us, the sale is often, in effect, already made. They've decided who they want to buy from, so some of the companies they contact are just part of their due diligence. They're ensuring that they are making the right decision. It's highly unlikely that these companies will win their business. When we aren't including P2P prospecting as one of our key sales strategies, these pre-sold customers make up the majority of our customer interactions, so it makes sense that we fall into the trap of believing that there's no point in trying to sell to customers who have presumably already made an informed purchasing decision. When we make assumptions about how well informed our customers are, we imagine ourselves at their mercy. The customer has all the information they need, so we willingly cede them all the power as well.

These traps have sprung, and too many of us have accepted that we salespeople have to get used to life in the new paradigm. Nearly all of today's B2B businesses are falling into these traps, and very few are extricating themselves. They are either over-dependent, or they are sliding down the slippery slope, well on their way to becoming over-dependent on their websites and online marketing campaigns to generate all of the new enquiries for their sales teams to sell to.

As reliance on our online presence to generate sales leads has grown, so too has online competition. Prospects looking for our products or services online may once have had a handful of options to choose from; now, they have dozens or perhaps more. We risk getting lost in the crowd, so we are spending more and more money trying to win a place on the first page of Google's search results—and for diminishing returns. The vast majority of B2B Sales Directors and business owners that I talk to tell me the same story: the number and quality of sales enquiries they receive each week has either plateaued or is dropping (often precipitously). Their sales teams are being asked to do more with less. They're treading water in increasingly choppy seas.

And the traps themselves aren't even the worst of it. Here's the biggest problem: your competitors have fallen into the same traps you have. They are using exactly the same online marketing strategies, and they are competing for the same customers you are trying to win. Your competitors have a great website, just like you do. They are using SEO and AdWords to drive prospects to their websites, just like you are. They re-design their website a month or two after you do yours. Theirs uses slightly more effective SEO or AdWords strategies, and you're back to the drawing board—back to jamming keywords into your content, back to focusing more of your efforts on marketing than on sales, back to trying to regain the razor-thin digital edge over your competitors.

We're now focusing so much on online marketing that we're suffering from observational bias, or what is sometimes called the streetlight effect. Because we're so focused on the prospects we think we can convert quickly, we've come to believe that the prospects who are making online enquiries are the *only* prospects out there. We're missing the vast majority of our potential prospects—they are in the shadows. They're not in the streetlights, they're outside of what we've chosen to illuminate, so we've stopped noticing them entirely. The more tightly we focus our beam on easy-to-win customers, the less likely it is we will see the potential customers that lie in the shadows.

The people who are looking online for our products or services are only the tip of our iceberg. It's understandable that we are expending a great deal of energy chasing these prospects: they have a clear and often expressed need for what we're selling. If they've already seen our name online or have even a passing familiarity with what we sell or do, we should be doing everything we can to win their business. The mistake is to believe that these are the *only* prospects worth pursuing.

What about the people who need what you're selling but, for whatever reason, don't find you? What about those who have resigned themselves to the idea that their situation or problem is unsolvable and have therefore stopped looking for solutions? What about those who need what you are selling but haven't had the time or inclination to start looking for a solution? What about those who just don't know that you exist or that you can help them? When you add these groups together, they add up to a much larger potential market than the one you're probably targeting right now. These are the prospects that form the bulk of your iceberg. They sit beneath the waterline, and they represent as much as 80% of your potential market. But we've all become so focused on the 20% of the iceberg that's above the waterline that we've forgotten that there's a much larger market out there, and we've forgotten how important this larger market is to the success of our business. Critically, we've forgotten how to find these prospects and how to engage them in dialogue.

When you start looking beneath the waterline, you'll start to identify and contact potential customers before your competitors can see them. We've all been a prospect that sits below the waterline at some point. We've all been less than satisfied or even downright unhappy with something, but we live with it, sometimes for months, sometimes for years before we decide to take action. At home it might be a swimming pool cleaner that has developed a "memory" and only cleans the same part of the pool each day. It might be a lawnmower that takes 10 minutes to start each time you use it. Or perhaps it is an Internet service that frequently drops out and frequently needs to be rebooted. The same is true at work: perhaps you are still using underperforming software or making do with a CRM system that doesn't synch appointments with your calendars correctly, or you might be needlessly spending hours preparing reports every week or grinning and bearing it each time a troublesome piece of equipment breaks down or doesn't do what it is meant to.

At some point, something snaps. You've had enough, so you start looking for solutions. You go online and start looking for an answer to your problem. It's at this point that you go from being submerged to emerged and, based on what you find (and, indirectly, on what you don't find), you make a buying decision quickly—usually within a few days.

What if someone had called you before you started looking online? What if they had told you they had a solution to your problem before you'd reached your breaking point? Chances are you would have heard them out, met with them, and, provided the solution looked appropriate, you'd have rewarded them with your business. If the salesperson made you feel comfortable and did a good job presenting their product and its features, you might even make your purchase without going online to look at alternatives. In this case, you would never have even appeared at the tip of the iceberg for any of that supplier's competitors. The sale was made while you were, to all intents and purposes, invisible. This is the power of selling beneath the waterline: its ability to make the invisible visible.

The alternative is to continue scrabbling for the same customers that your competitors are talking to. Going this route isn't getting any easier. Because there are so many competitors piling on, selling to the tip of the iceberg is becoming more and more difficult (that is, time-consuming and expensive). It's more difficult than it once was to appear above the fold on the first page of search results, and realistically, if you're not above the fold, you're not getting noticed. If you're below the fold, your competitors are king of the hill, and you're probably scrambling to keep up. If you're not on the first page, you're probably going to start taking on water (if you're not doing so already).

To make things harder still, advertising space is at a premium. There are now only four paid adverts at the top of each search page. This drives up rates, making it more and more expensive to get to the top of the page and stay there. In this environment (and in the traps I've described above) remaining competitive online means spending more money to get, at best, the same results as you used to.

The trickle of qualified leads being fed to your sales team gets smaller and smaller. The phones aren't ringing, and sales numbers are stagnant or declining. There starts to be talk about the "good old days"—the days when online marketing campaigns could be relied upon to produce an avalanche of prospects. Your sales team—as talented as they might be—has all but forgotten how to find their own leads. They know how to massage the leads they're getting from online marketing campaigns, but not much else.

In his excellent book on organisational and personal change, *Who Moved My Cheese?*, Spencer Johnson says that when something changes, we are often slow to recognise it at first. We live in denial in an inflexible, mouse-like mindset. "I found my cheese here," we tell ourselves, "so it will always be here". Even when the cheese is no longer there, or there is less than there once was, we keep going back to the same place, looking for the same cheese and assuming things will eventually go back to the way they once were. What's happening in sales is a great example of this. We still believe that online marketing is the way for us to win our sales, hit our sales targets and grow. But things have changed. The cheese has moved. If we want to be successful in today's highly competitive B2B sales arena, we need to start looking for the cheese in new places. In other words, we need to go and find our own prospects instead of waiting for them to come to us.

The longer we continue to rely mainly or entirely on online marketing, the more crowded the tip of our iceberg becomes. Sales become harder to come by, and the pressure from above starts to mount. The sales team is asked and expected to do more—and often with less. They respond with complaints about the quantity or quality of the leads Marketing is providing them with. It's at this point that companies often begin to think about ramping up their prospecting efforts, but they encounter resistance. Tell today's salespeople to start digging, and you'll probably be met with more than a few blank stares, and perhaps outright hostility. "How and who do we call?" they'll ask. "Cold calling", they say, "is a massive waste of time."

But P2P prospecting is not a waste of time; it is, on the contrary, an essential part of sales (albeit a largely forgotten one). If you want to take control of and improve your sales figures, you need to bring P2P prospecting back into your sales process. You need to use a proactive approach to prospecting, one that lets you see below the waterline and start talking to the potential customers that your competitors don't yet know exist. Do this and you will soon start seeing steadily climbing sales figures.

WE NEED MARKETING

Your customers are out there and you know it. Your analytics are probably telling you that there are hundreds or even thousands of visits to your website each month, so there are clearly prospects out there. For whatever reason, though, you're not getting through to them. Is the answer yet another website overhaul? Perhaps that will increase the very small percentage of visitors who are converted into concrete prospects. Perhaps it won't.

We need to stop thinking that Marketing (particularly their online efforts) can deliver all of the leads that Sales needs. We've been putting all our eggs in one basket for too long, relying far too heavily on marketers emailing to do the job that was once done by salespeople prospecting. It's time to stop looking at common practice as the best possible practice. Just because everyone else is doing it doesn't mean it's the right thing to do.

Now, don't get me wrong, I'm not putting down online marketing (or any marketing for that matter). It's important. Actually, it's a vital component of any company's sales and marketing strategy. When you do it well, it does deliver well-primed sales leads. Marketing also defines and reinforces your brand and what you stand for. It creates offers and communicates these with your customers, prospects and the larger market. Nowhere is this more important than online, where potential customers are searching for the solutions you are offering. Marketing is the lure that attracts curious consumers to your website, educating them and persuading them to call you. This includes your website (the Digital-Age shopfront), which is where people learn about what you sell, but also about your mission, your team and your values.

And here's the thing: the work and investment you've put into developing your website isn't wasted—far from it. The people you'll be prospecting to will go to your website to check you out before they meet with you. Your online presence will remain a vital part of your prospecting strategy. Having good online content builds credibility, positioning you as a subject matter expert and problem-solver. Ignore this as part of your strategy and you'll have trouble converting into customers the new prospects you discover beneath the waterline.

Marketing and Sales go hand in hand, and the last thing you want to do is throw the baby out with the bathwater. Marketing's brand-enhancing efforts are a crucial part of any good sales strategy. What we're doing by adding P2P prospecting is introducing new potential customers to your marketing messages and then using conversations to reinforce these messages. Not all of these prospects will purchase immediately, so ongoing marketing efforts will ensure you are front of mind when the prospect is ready to make their purchasing decision.

Your competitors put identical (or nearly identical) efforts into their website and their marketing campaigns, so to really get an edge on them, you need to do what they aren't doing or won't do. They're getting lost in the clutter, but your dedicated and proactive prospecting strategy will cut through this clutter. Your marketing messages will be more relevant and the open and click-through rates will be higher as a result.

We've all seen the numbers. Open and click-through rates are declining. The vast majority of email newsletters and articles that we are sending to prospects are not being read. Prospects are being inundated with these messages, and they're simply too busy to open them until they're facing an acute need.

Good online marketing (for example, top-shelf content and eye-catching email campaigns) is much more likely to lead to higher open and click-through rates, but this can't be the only strategy you have in place to find and build relationships with prospects. When I say that we need to bring back P2P prospecting, I'm not saying we need to shutter Marketing and online customer outreach. We *need* Marketing. But we also need to combine our successful marketing strategies with new (or perhaps older) methods of engaging customers in dialogue. We need to bring P2P prospecting back into our sales process.

Chapter summary

- The Internet has dramatically changed the sales landscape.

- Online marketing has come to dominate the early stages of the sales process.

- Person-to-person (P2P) prospecting has been almost entirely abandoned.

- We have fallen into two traps:

  1. Assuming that online marketing can deliver to Sales all the prospects it needs
  2. Assuming that today's savvy B2B customers have all the information they need to make an informed purchasing decision.

- Your competitors are doing the same things you are, so you're all fighting to control the tip of the iceberg.

- Open and click-through rates are declining. We need a strategy that does not replace but, rather, complements our online marketing efforts.

- The solution is P2P prospecting, which lets us dive beneath the waterline to access a much larger potential market.

Chapter 2
BELOW THE WATERLINE

I F you're relying exclusively or almost exclusively on online marketing to bring you new customers, the prospects you're fighting the hardest to win represent only 20% of your market and they are the ones that all of your competitors are fighting for too. As I've said earlier, the prospects that find you online represent the tip of your iceberg—the part that floats above the water and is visible. These are the prospects who have filled in an online form or given you their email address. They might have downloaded a whitepaper, or called you out of the blue. They are today's hot prospects, the ones that your sales team can sell to today. And if they don't buy today, your marketing and sales team will work together to nurture them until they are ready to buy. These are fantastic prospects, but they only make up 20% of your market.

So what about the other 80% of your market? What about the customers who form the rest of your iceberg—those who are submerged below the waterline? They aren't looking for you and, what is worse, your sales team isn't looking for or finding them. These prospects don't know about you or what you're selling. They don't know that your product can fix a problem they have or that it can improve their business. They may not even know that you exist.

They may be working with one of your competitors without knowing that you could actually be doing a much better job for them. After all, when they bought from your competitor, they didn't do so thinking that they were buying the worst or even the second-best available solution. Their research led them to your competitor, and your competitor was able to convince them at that time that their solution was perfect for them. Unless they've encountered serious difficulties with your competitor's solution, chances are that they stopped looking the moment your competitor converted them into a customer. For as long as they think their needs are being met, no amount of SEO will help you reach these potential customers.

Writing these prospects off dramatically diminishes your target market. Though they might be working with your competitors today, they are still potential prospects for your sales team. You have something to offer that your competitors don't: your product, your customer service and your systems. These prospects may well need you (they just don't know it yet). These prospects are just one part of the much larger market that is not visible to you or your sales team right now. Your potential market is larger than you think, and it's full of potential new clients who are ripe for the picking. And here's the best part: nobody else is thinking about them, nobody else is talking to them because they don't know who these prospects are either. Nobody is looking below the tip of their iceberg.

Prospecting in the right way is what's going to show you more—much more—than the tip of your iceberg. In what follows, I'll be showing you how to find these potential customers and make yourself more visible to them. They'll be seeing your messages (often for the first time), and you'll be building relationships that will translate, in time, to a steady stream of new business. No more waiting for the phone to ring (now your sales team will be making the calls); no more hoping that potential customers will find their way to your website (your sales team will be taking them by the hand and leading them there). P2P prospecting is going to help you dive beneath the waterline, where you can first see and then reach out to entirely new groups of potential customers, engaging them in two-way conversations that are more personalised than even the most sophisticated and compelling marketing materials ever could be.

There was a time not too long ago when sales prospecting of the kind we'll be discussing in this book was a central strategy in the sales process. It was aggressive, proactive and constant. Online marketing has replaced this with less-intrusive prospecting and, thanks to the success of early adopters, telephone prospecting was written off as a sales relic. With so few organisations using P2P prospecting to reach their markets, decision makers are no longer facing a barrage of daily sales calls. This means that they are far more open to high-quality P2P prospecting calls. Aggressive prospecting calls have fallen by the wayside, and it was right to discard them. They were more harmful to our brand than they were helpful in terms of sales numbers, but this doesn't mean that prospecting has outlived its usefulness. By addressing your newly discovered groups of prospects warmly, politely and engagingly, you'll be opening the door to mutually productive relationships—and lots of them.

Just how much latent potential is there in the market that sits below the waterline? What would accessing and selling to this market mean to your bottom line? Here are just some of the benefits:

- Your sales team starts speaking to four times as many prospects as they have in the past. Each year, your sales team meets and exceeds stretch targets (that is, targets you previously thought were out of reach).

- You have predictable sales performance every month—no more peaks and troughs, just steady growth.
- The more your team prospects, the more opportunities come to you through referrals.
- You're back in control of your sales pipeline and are no longer reliant on online marketing to deliver all of the sales leads for your sales team.
- You are selling to prospects who have not been shopping around for what you sell, so they are much more likely to buy from you than from your competitors.
- There is less pressure on price as these prospects haven't been out there shopping around and talking to your competitors.
- Your company gains market share steadily until you become number one in its market.

Because you're looking below the waterline, you're also selling to a much bigger market. You're leaving your competitors behind you. You're changing the playing field and the rules of engagement. You're doing what nobody else will do: proactively searching out prospects rather than waiting for them to find you. You're building relationships before the customer reaches the point where they are considering a purchase, before they start doing their research. By doing so, you're putting yourself in pole position, poised to win their business when they are ready to buy.

You're doing the work that lets you jump ahead of your competitors, standing out in the market. You're beginning a relationship with your future clients much earlier in their buyer's journey and so, when they are ready to buy, they will be substantially less likely to even consider your competitors, and if they do consider them, they are still more likely to buy from you because you have built a relationship with them over time. Regular person-to-person conversations mean that they have come to know and trust you. You gain a huge competitive edge because you are doing what the vast majority of businesses in your industry aren't doing.

CONSISTENT, LONG-TERM, AND STRATEGIC

With the diminishing returns of online marketing, some companies have quietly started exploring prospecting. Those few B2B companies that can tell which way the wind is blowing have started looking below the waterline and are beginning to talk to the prospects who form the submerged part of their iceberg. They are finding new prospects before these potential customers even start their search for their products or services, and this is helping them win business that would otherwise go to their competitors. However, very few of these companies are using prospecting strategically. They may be prospecting, and they may even be enjoying some success, but they're still not winning as much business as they could be.

Why? Because, while P2P prospecting might be straightforward, it's not easy. It is simple to understand, but, unless approached in the right way, it is hard to execute. For most companies, sales prospecting tends to be stop-start. They prospect for a month or two and then allow it to taper off. Their pipeline is flowing again, so they start to focus on massaging the best leads they've fed into their pipeline and on delivery. The minute they start to pull away from their competitors, they take their foot off the accelerator.

The trick is to keep driving forward with your eyes focused on the horizon. The most successful sales prospecting campaigns are consistently applied long-term strategies. My rule of thumb, gained from over 10 years of prospecting experience, is that you need to be prospecting in the right way for at least six months (and, depending on what you're selling and to whom, perhaps more) before you start seeing real results. You might see results earlier in your campaign, but these are just a taste of what's to come. The larger goal is to build momentum, and momentum kicks in for most companies at around the five to six-month period.

Don't let early or mid-stage successes divert your course. To truly realise your full potential, you need to keep going, even when you're beginning to reap what you have sown. Too often, just when they are starting to see positive results, companies turn their attention to dealing with the new sales they have just generated, letting their prospecting fall by the wayside. Within a few months or even weeks their sales pipeline is empty again. They've lost, not just the three to six months of sales opportunities that their prospecting would have turned up, but also the time it takes them to reactivate the prospecting process.

Companies who do their own prospecting typically hire a dedicated telemarketer, get their sales team to do their own prospecting, or they assign prospecting to an existing staff member as an additional duty. But regardless of which option they choose, they provide little training and very little supervision, thinking that prospecting is a straightforward enough task. After a couple of months, they either aren't getting any sales leads, or they're getting leads they don't want (that is, unqualified or unreceptive ones).

At this point, they try a different option—often reassigning the task to a hired or outsourced dedicated prospector. With minimal guidance, the results with the new prospector are less than overwhelming. They soon find themselves back at square one, with little to show for their efforts and expense. Because they all start the same, these stories have predictable endings as well: within four to six months give or take, the company has given up on prospecting entirely.

Other companies engage an outside provider, only to give up the strategy after as little as a few weeks because they haven't seen an immediate spike in sales. This is an expectations problem. The prospecting sales cycle moves more slowly than the one we have become accustomed to. Rather than days or weeks, the P2P prospecting sales cycle lasts three to six months or perhaps more. Expecting the sales to come pouring in within the first few weeks is unrealistic. A lack of patience and unreasonable expectations cut far too many prospecting campaigns short prematurely—long before they have the chance to prove themselves.

To be successful, telephone prospecting demands an investment of time. Just as you're not going to win big with an SEO strategy if you only run it for a week or a month, P2P prospecting isn't going to generate the kind of long-term results you want without a significant time investment. A few hours a week for a few weeks isn't going to amount to much of anything. The secret to success in sales is (and always has been) consistent and strategic activity, day after day, week after week.

The best salespeople in the world understand this. They meet with new prospects every day, and they never stop introducing themselves to new potential customers. A brimming pipeline is the result of long-term diligence; it's not the work of a week or a month or even a quarter. It's an ongoing work—one that relies upon momentum, perpetually driving forward rather than resting on its laurels.

But most sales professionals have forgotten that hard work is what drives our bottom line. We've allowed ourselves to be lulled into a false sense of security, believing that the Internet will do all the work for us. We've convinced ourselves that all we need to do to get sales is to hang out our digital banner. For a time, that was enough, but that time has passed. The days when we could meet our targets while selling to only 20% of our market are behind us. As I keep saying, it's time to look beneath the waterline and start selling to our entire iceberg.

At my company, Forrest Marketing Group, we specialise in B2B sales prospecting. Over the last decade, we've made more than four million phone calls on behalf of our clients. We've generated tens of thousands of sales leads, which have turned into hundreds of millions of dollars in sales for our clients. These sales have been the result of getting below the waterline and prospecting to potential customers who weren't on our clients' radars. We have introduced many of these customers to our clients for the first time. Almost all of the sales leads we have generated were not looking for our client's services online when we called them. They were unseen in online marketing terms. But they turned into sales for our clients, and thanks to the strategy's continued success, P2P prospecting has become a key part of our clients' sales and marketing strategies.

Is there a possibility that our clients would have won this business on their own when the customer started searching online? Perhaps, but by getting out in front of that search, we put our clients in pole position, well ahead of their competitors. We showed them how to play the long game, and they won more business because they did so. When the flag dropped, they were in the driving seat with the engine already running. Their competitors were still looking for their keys.

SHIFTING GEARS

A few years ago, I bought a car—the first brand new car I had purchased. I'd always driven a manual, but the salesman talked me into a hybrid automatic-manual transmission. The modern gearbox was, the salesman told me, the only way to drive, offering the best of both worlds: all the convenience of automatic when you need it, and all the engine control of the manual transmission.

He told me I would love it once I got used to the paddles on the steering column, but by the end of the first month it was clear that I had made a mistake. I hated the gearbox, and I hated the flappy paddles on the steering column. The engine was never in the gear I wanted it to be in. In its automatic setting, it downshifted or upshifted, seemingly at random, or it stubbornly stayed in the wrong gear when I wanted it to change. I tried to get used to it, but I longed for my old manual transmission. I am, it turns out, a dyed-in-the-wool manual transmission guy.

I lived with this car for more than a year, and, all through that time, I was dissatisfied, but I did nothing, hoping that the automatic gearbox would grow on me. I stuck with my purchase because I had only just bought it and, partly as well, because I knew I would lose money if I tried to trade it in so early into my lease. Every time the gearbox did something I didn't want it to, I would just grin and bear it. I reached the breaking point one day when I needed to change gears in the middle of a roundabout. The paddles (which had turned with the wheel) were no longer at 9 o'clock and 3 o'clock on the steering wheel, where I expected them to be. I slammed my palms into the steering wheel in frustration. I had had enough.

When I got to the office that day, the first thing I did was call my finance broker to ask him if there was any way to sell the car without taking a bath on the loan. He chuckled and said it probably wasn't possible, but he'd check to see if there was any wiggle room. Within an hour, he called back. It turned out I could sell the car and purchase a new one without losing very much on the loan. I had a new car (one with a good, old-fashioned manual gearbox) within ten days.

How does this story relate to the iceberg? I drove a car that I didn't like for more than a year. I drove it every day of that year, yet I did nothing to address the issue until that dislike became an intense hatred. We all do similar things, and it is helpful to remember this when considering your market. They are living with their pain. It's only when this pain becomes unbearable that they do something about it. They start researching and looking at their options. When they've reached this stage, they (like me) are often desperate for a solution.

They become the tip-of-the-iceberg customers we've all been targeting, and we know that they often find a solution remarkably quickly, doing their own research online and leaving little time for intervention. These are the informed customers who have changed the sales landscape, and we need to remember that their pain or need didn't materialise out of thin air. There was a long period before these prospects became desperate—a period when they were ideal prospects but were still submerged beneath the waterline. It's only when their annoyance reached its boiling point that they became a visible part of our iceberg.

What about my situation? What if a finance broker had called me out of the blue when I'd only had the car for three months to see if there was anything she could do for me? If she'd asked me about my situation, I gladly would have told her about how much I hated the car. If she had shown me she could help me get into another car without it costing too much on the loan, she would have won me as a customer. I wouldn't have described myself as a potential customer at that point, but I still would have become her client had she approached me proffering the right solution. I might not have bought from her there and then; I might have left it for a month or two more, but she had planted the seed and would be in pole position when I was ready to purchase, which would have been well before I became desperate. Having planted that seed, it would have germinated well before I became desperate. Discomfort or frustration would have been enough.

The same is true for your future customers. You have what they need to solve their issues; they just don't know it yet, and you just don't know them yet. The way you change that is by finding them even when they are sitting out of sight below the waterline and beginning a conversation with them, and the way you do that is through P2P prospecting.

Chapter summary

- The prospects who are submerged below your waterline make up as much as 80% of your potential market.

- They might not know who you are, or they might be working with your competitors, but writing them off for these reasons is limiting your business's potential.

- P2P prospecting will help you gain market share, put you in control of your sales pipeline (making your sales performance predictable), and help you meet and exceed your sales targets.

- For a prospecting strategy to be effective it must be consistent, long-term, and strategic.

- A lack of patience and unrealistic expectations scuttle far too many prospecting campaigns before they can really bear fruit. Remember, a prospecting campaign will need three to six months to build momentum.

- P2P prospecting is the best way to uncover issues. It is the only way to initiate conversations with prospects before they become visible to your competitors.

- You have what your customers want or need; they just don't know it yet.

Chapter 3
THE LOST ART
OF P2P PROSPECTING

P2P prospecting is how you get below the waterline and start selling to your entire iceberg. It's not easy, but that means your competitors probably aren't doing it—and if they are, they're not doing it effectively or strategically. Put it to work for you and you will quickly jump ahead of them.

Bring new techniques and new energy to your prospecting and results will be close to immediate. This won't mean that you'll be doubling your sales overnight, but it will mean that your sales team will start meeting with new prospects within as little as a few days, and they'll be talking to potential customers who your competitors *aren't* talking to—namely, those who haven't been looking online.

Sales will follow, but how long will this take? That will depend on your sales cycle. New prospects in your funnel will mean more sales, but that doesn't necessarily translate to faster sales. If it normally takes six months to make a sale, it will probably take at least that long (if not longer) for new prospects to move through the funnel. Remember, you are engaging with prospects earlier than you normally would, so it will probably take longer to make sales. P2P prospecting is not a short-term strategy. It is not a quick fix. It is a long-term strategy that, when implemented correctly, will boost sales performance and continually deliver great sales to your business for years to come.

At my company, as you can imagine, we spend a lot of time prospecting— for ourselves. It would be strange if we didn't. Our sales cycle from inbound enquiries is typically quite fast, averaging around four weeks from initial contact to a sale being made. For our P2P prospecting leads, however, the sales cycle is longer—typically around 90 days. We still know, however, within around four weeks whether or not a sale is going to be made. At that point it's no longer a question of *if* but *when.*

Companies have to go through a number of steps before they are ready to buy, such as gaining internal approval and budget. If they are a tip-of-the-iceberg prospect (one who is already searching online for what we're selling) they have already completed these steps. However, when we prospect to them, they have not reached that point yet. They haven't yet considered the solution we're presenting to them. That means they haven't yet got a budget or approval. So, they have to take these steps *after* our initial call and meeting, which means that the sales cycle for these prospects is longer than it is for the tip-of-the-iceberg ones.

But here's the thing: seven out of ten of the prospects who decide to use our services tell us that they are not considering anyone else to look after their prospecting calls for them. We are the *only* supplier they are considering. If you're like me, you'll be more than happy to trade a slightly longer sales cycle for the chance to be the only supplier being considered.

Today's sales-driven organisations have lost sight of the importance of proactive P2P prospecting. Those salespeople who have been around since the pre-digital age don't want to go back to P2P prospecting, and those who've never tried it are, like so many prospects, full of objections. They say:

- "Prospecting takes far too long to yield results."
- "Prospecting doesn't work."
- "Prospecting is too hard. I don't even know where to begin."
- "I'm busy with other things. I don't have the time to prospect."
- "Who would I even call?"
- "I don't know how to deal with objections."
- "I don't know how to start a conversation with a cold prospect on the phone."

In the chapters that follow, I will answer all of these objections, and I'll show you how to prospect in ways that will make your results more than worth your efforts. As you start to see results coming in and you begin to outperform your competition and even become the top seller in your market, your competitors—who still aren't willing to prospect proactively—will struggle to take back the market share that you have won from them. They won't do what you are willing to do. They won't invest the time and energy to see below the waterline and to uncover their entire iceberg.

Prospecting really only takes two things: knowledge and discipline. You hold the former in your hands. You'll need to share what you learn in this book with your sales team, who will probably need training as well as support and management from you (especially with the cold calling). But also, if they aren't used to selling to this type of prospect, they may also struggle at first with their sales meetings. Selling to cold prospects means having a conversation that is often very unlike the ones they've probably been having with the warm or hot leads that they're used to dealing with from online enquiries and referrals. In their initial meeting with cold call prospects, they'll have to learn to grab the prospect's attention, to generate interest and to uncover issues. For most of them, this will mean training and learning a new approach to their sales meetings, on top of learning how to prospect the right way.

Knowledge isn't going to make much of a difference without discipline. P2P prospecting—like other long-term strategies—demands nothing less than a fully committed and lasting effort. The system contained in this book needs to be applied consistently every day for months on end. Stay disciplined and you will leap so far ahead of your competitors that they will all but disappear from your rear-view mirror. It'll be easy to remain disciplined when you start glimpsing your market's true potential and you discover the wealth of companies that lie beneath the waterline. Stay the course. Before long, you'll be generating sales from pools of prospects that your competitors don't even know exist.

THE CONVERSATION AT THE HEART OF THE SALE

A truly successful prospecting programme is one that puts the conversation at the heart of the sale. This is something that many companies have either chosen to ignore or have forgotten entirely. A conversation does what nothing else can; it engages prospects in two-way dialogue, building trust and finding common ground. It's the best way to uncover issues and communicate solutions. Conversation presents the prospector with the unique opportunity to tailor the selling message to each prospect's specific situation and specific needs, making it a powerful sales tool unlike any other.

This is what online marketing (and the sales approaches that have come in its wake) have lost sight of: the personal touch. With the advent of email, digital marketing and marketing automation, we have become over-reliant on electronic communication. Too often, we only connect with prospects electronically. The conversation—if it happens at all—is coming later and later in the sales process, and we're missing the chance to start the relationship off on the right foot and to position ourselves as the front-runner to win the sale.

This is part of a broader communication trend. Textual communication has taken the place of verbal conversation. This is even true with our friends. How often do your friends call you at home? How often do you use your mobile to talk to someone—and I do mean *talking* to them (texting doesn't count). How many of your friends, relatives, and colleagues only hear from you via text, Facebook or email? If you're like most citizens of the Digital Age, your answers to these questions are probably *never, almost never,* and *too many.*

When mobile phones first became common, conversations were suddenly everywhere. They were out in the open like never before. I can remember sitting in the lobby of a five-star hotel in Manila and listening to the noise around me. Hotel lobbies, once quiet places, were suddenly awash with the cacophony of overlapping conversations. The noise was almost too much to handle, but at least people were talking to each other. The room was alive.

Fast forward to today. When was the last time you heard someone having a proper conversation on their phone. Sure, people still do this, but they spend far more time texting, emailing, checking in and posting than they do talking. It's the same thing in business. We rely on emails far more than phone calls for our communication. They're cheap, fast, and easy. It makes sense, but in the movement from oral to textual communication, something's been lost—particularly in sales.

Admittedly, what has been lost has been replaced with something *almost* as powerful: the Internet and its powerful communication tools have, without a doubt, proved to be the most life-changing and business-changing invention of the last century. Whether we want to communicate with a single person or thousands, the process takes seconds. We send a marketing message to a vast network of people and, just like that, software can tell us how many people have opened the message, how many have clicked through to a whitepaper or other article or to our website.

We can know with some certainty whether or not our marketing messages are being received, but, as a way of communicating with prospects, email marketing tells us very little else. This means that, as a means of communication, it is not as effective as the conversation.

These days, click through rates are typically south of 5%. In their June 2016 edition, MailerMailer analysed data compiled from almost one billion opt-in email newsletters. They reported that the average click through rate in 2015 was just 1.9%. That means 98.1% of emails being sent are not getting a response. Response rates, where a prospect actually reaches out to contact you as a direct result of an e-marketing campaign, are even lower than this—often in the sub-Arctic regions.

The general mood in sales departments is one of complacence. When a prospect doesn't buy immediately, or at least fairly quickly, they get placed into an automated nurturing process. Our marketing automation software takes over and nurtures these prospects in the background, using emails, e-newsletters and other electronic messages until they are ready to buy (or until they ask to be removed from the list).

This sounds great in theory. It saves time and effort, but it takes away the responsibility for selling from the sales team. Instead of actively selling and managing their own sales pipeline, today's salespeople often don't get involved until marketing tells them that, according to the marketing software, a prospect has reached a certain threshold.

The prospect is, if not ready to buy, at least in the decision-making stages of their journey, and it is time for Sales to intervene. Sales leaps to the helm and engages the prospect. I'm not denying the ease and seductiveness of this process, but I am questioning its long-term efficaciousness. With open and click through rates declining, salespeople need to take the initiative once again. They need to start and maintain conversations, and they need to do so while the prospect is still below the waterline. Once they've started the conversation, marketing automation software can be brought in to nurture these prospects, but there should still be ongoing P2P conversations, and these should form the central platform for the sales process. On this platform, you'll be placing submerged and recently emerged prospects.

The submerged prospects may be those who haven't yet responded to the messages being sent by Marketing. They might not be receiving anything from you at all, and if they are receiving your marketing messages, they are probably getting similar generic information from your competitors. You don't really know about them (yet) and they really don't really know much about you (yet). It's time to start proactively selling to these people, and this begins when we remember that selling is about more than closing just the easy opportunities. At its best, selling not only pushes at open doors, it also creates doors where there were walls. It does this through relationship-building, and there's no better way to build a good relationship than through a conversation. In what follows, I'll help you bring the art of the conversation back into the sales process. You learn how to place your salespeople (and the conversations they have) at the heart of the sale—which is right where they should be.

Proactive P2P prospecting means bringing dialogue back into the first contact with each new prospect and ensuring that it also forms part of the ongoing nurturing process. It makes person-to-person conversation integral to the relationship between the organisation and the customer. There is power in the written word, but there is greater power in the spoken word, far greater again in the dialogue between two people. We have forgotten how to have a well-crafted initial sales conversation—at least partly because we have forgotten just how effective this can be in terms of uncovering opportunities and getting prospects to realise, first, that they have a problem and, second, that we have the solution.

Conversation becomes especially powerful when used in conjunction with automated marketing. It's important to understand that P2P prospecting on its own is not the answer, any more than automated marketing is. Both are important sales tools, and they need to be used together. When we start including conversations at key points in the sales process, we make it more likely that our automated marketing messages will be opened and read. When we combine the strengths of Sales and Marketing, together they will deliver powerful growth and consistent sales for the company.

So, just to be clear, relying solely on conversations is not the solution I'm proposing in this book. We need to make use of *all* the tools available to us, and conversation-based selling is one of these tools. It is, in fact, an extremely important sales tool that has been neglected. It's gathering dust in the corner of the workshop, but it's still serviceable. All we need to do is pick it up, dust it off, and put it back to work for us. The time has come to rediscover the power of conversation and place it back at the heart of the sales process.

LEAKY AS A SIEVE

Thanks to its ability to build stronger relationships between the organisation and the prospect, P2P prospecting can dramatically improve your pipeline efficiency. According to Martin Walsh, Chief Marketing and Digital Officer at Ansarada, 70% of the prospects that sit in our sales funnel will leak out, simply due to a lack of P2P follow-up on the part of salespeople. However, 86% of the prospects who leak out in this way will buy what we are trying to sell them at some point (though not necessarily from us). In other words, the 86% of prospects that leak out of pipeline have a need for what we sell, but it's not an immediate need. By failing to follow up consistently, salespeople let these great prospects go and once they've been let go, we run the risk of losing them to our competitors.

When salespeople assume (and they often do) that they can rely on marketing software to maintain a relationship with their prospects, they stop thinking about maintaining their long-term sales pipeline. They stop owning it. They hand it off to marketing, assuming that ripe prospects will simply come back to them when they are ready to buy. The focus of the sales team is on the next hot lead to pop their head above the waterline.

This creates a hands-off mindset that leaves a sales pipeline as leaky as a sieve: "If someone buys from me," the thinking goes, "that's great. If not, I'll leave it to Marketing to nurture. Surely, there'll be another hot lead coming along any moment now anyway. And if there isn't, that's no fault of mine. I'll just sit here and look busy, waiting for the next hot lead to land on my desk." If this mindset were conducive to success, I wouldn't be writing this book. If we had an endless supply of hot opportunities, each one more primed to purchase than the last, you probably wouldn't be reading this book. But we don't. Nobody does. Everyone who is in business today has a finite number of prospects. The more niched you are, the smaller your supply of sales-ready prospects.

The proliferation of this hands-off approach to nurturing by salespeople means that most prospects are receiving daily floods of impersonal and only partially relevant marketing messages. In the main, they're ignoring the vast majority of these. We don't have to look very far to verify this. We have all been, at some time or another, a prospect for someone, somewhere, and we all have strategies to help us avoid unwanted solicitation. Maybe it's a second email address that you use when you sign up to a newsletter, whitepaper, or other special offer online. You probably use this email address so that the daily bombardment of marketing emails doesn't distract you from more urgent messages. Even when we do give out our primary email address (perhaps because the organisation is one we imagine ourselves one day doing business with), it's only a matter of time before we stop reading their marketing messages. The longer this continues, the more likely we are to unsubscribe and the less likely it is that we will engage in any way with the organisation or its salespeople. It's at this point that nurturing becomes pestering, and we've all experienced this as well.

Just have a look at some of the current statistics around email marketing. According to the January 2017 Email Marketing Benchmarks report published by Mail Chimp Research, open rates in 2016 varied between 15% and 29%, depending on industry. For most industries the figure was 20% to 25%. Click through rates were substantially lower than this, ranging between just 1.3% and 5.6%, with the average around 2%.

Data from MailerMailer supports this; the graph below shows declining click through rates over the last few years. In the first half of 2011, the average click through rate was 3.5%. By the second half of 2015, it had dropped to 1.9% (slightly higher than its 2014 low point, but still a 46% decline in just five years).

This means that, out of every 1,000 messages received, only 19 will lead to any action at all. A staggering 981 of them will do nothing at all. These numbers don't show any signs of improving in the foreseeable future. If anything, they'll continue to get worse.

Average click through rate between 2011 and 2015 (by half year)

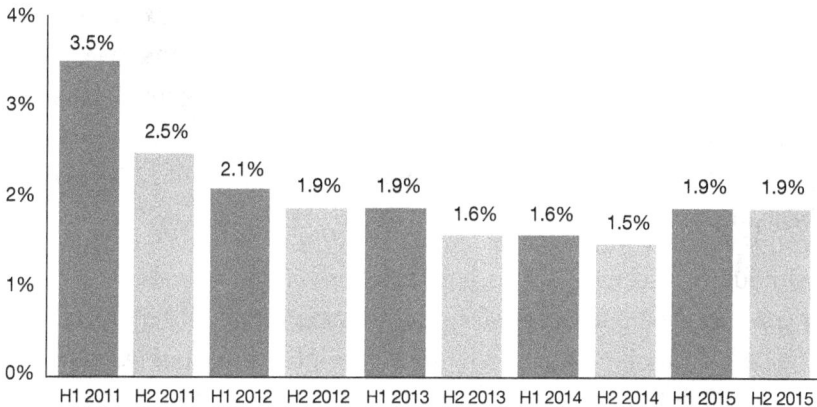

SEALING THE LEAKS

Marketing emails may be relatively inexpensive, and they may make reaching a large pool of prospects quite easy, but they are only marginally effective, and they will probably become less so with each passing year. It's a dramatically inefficient way to work with the prospects in your sales pipeline. Those who fall out by unsubscribing, or simply by ignoring and deleting your messages without reading them are unlikely to be amenable to being fed back into the system—unless, that is, you change your approach dramatically.

You might have found some success with e-marketing, and I'm not suggesting that you should stop addressing your market in this way. E-marketing campaigns are effective for exactly the reasons I have pointed out above: they are simple, inexpensive, and they give you nearly instant access to a broad audience. It is, however, worth asking yourself: What is e-marketing doing to help me create the kind of sales that will drive explosive growth? How much information is it helping me gather? What is it telling me about a prospect's potential of becoming a customer? What is it telling me about their budget, their problems, or their current solution? If you're like most companies, the answer to most of these questions is either *nothing* or *next to nothing*. That's because e-marketing, like most marketing, is a one-way street. You are giving information out, but you are not getting much back. To get that information, you need to start having conversations with your prospects—both brand new prospects and those who have already been in your sales pipeline for some time.

Without these conversations, your pipeline will never produce the sales it can and should be producing. The solution is right in front of us, but the combination of a continual trickle of inbound enquiries, plus the availability of marketing automation software to do all of the staying-in-touch work that salespeople used to do, has made us lazy. For too long we've taken the easy way out, and it's already starting to catch up with us. As pipelines dry up it's going to be the disciplined who find the most enviable success. They're the ones who understand that the sales worth getting don't come easy. Selling is, and always has been, hard work; it requires drive, determination and consistency. Any shortcut in sales is a shortcut to eventual failure.

A friend of mine is one of the top ten real estate agents in Australia. The secret to his success? He sees 15 new prospects every week. Every week. Not just some weeks, not three out of four weeks. Every week. He's able to convert many of these prospects to sales because he's dynamic and he knows how to get the best price for a property—both clearly factors in his success. But you can draw a straight line from his constantly replenished pipeline to his success. His personality and his salesmanship have next to no value if he is not meeting new prospects. Even if he were the best at selling real estate in the world, he wouldn't be half as successful as he is if he just sat around waiting for the phone to ring. Without a constantly replenished pipeline and the personal contact that is also a part of his approach, he wouldn't be where he is today. How does he get these prospects? A couple come from referrals, a few more from enquiries to the office, but the majority come from P2P prospecting.

It's time we put conversation back where it belongs: front and centre in the prospecting process. It's time to bring back the personal contact that our sales team used to have with our prospects. It's time to make this our default sales strategy. We have allowed the hype surrounding e-marketing to lull us into a false sense of security. We have been duped into thinking that conversations between the prospect and the organisation's representatives are unnecessary and can be replaced by impersonal digital content. We need to focus on having quality sales conversations at the beginning, during and at the end of the sales cycle, because people buy from people they like, not from emails they like.

What we need is to set up a system to uncover the whole of our iceberg, both the tip of it that sits above water and the huge mass below the waterline. Then we need to start talking with each of those prospects. And I do mean talking, and talking regularly. We will, by doing this, uncover prospects we didn't know we had, and we will go on to build a highly efficient sales pipeline that will be the envy of our competitors. Best of all, we will be making good sales today, tomorrow and all year round, year after year.

Of course we will still use e-marketing and marketing automation software; we just won't rely on it. We will talk to our prospects, find out about their individual needs, get them to know and like us, and then we will sell to them. When we do this, we can take complete control of the sales process and, with it, we can also begin to control the success of our business. Taking control in this way starts with gaining a more complete picture of our potential market, and that is exactly what we are going to start doing in the next section.

Chapter summary

- Whether they are new to the game or are seasoned professionals, today's salespeople don't feel much inclined to engage prospects through P2P prospecting.

- Successful prospecting boils down to just two things: knowledge and discipline.

- Successful P2P prospecting puts the conversation back at the heart of the prospecting process.

- The conversation is such a powerful selling tool because it gives the salesperson the ability to tailor the message to suit each prospect's particular needs and issues.

- Selling is about uncovering and creating opportunities, not just taking orders from interested shoppers.

- Impersonal and widely dispersed marketing messages are proving to be increasingly ineffective.

- More effective by far is a personal approach that includes person-to-person conversations.

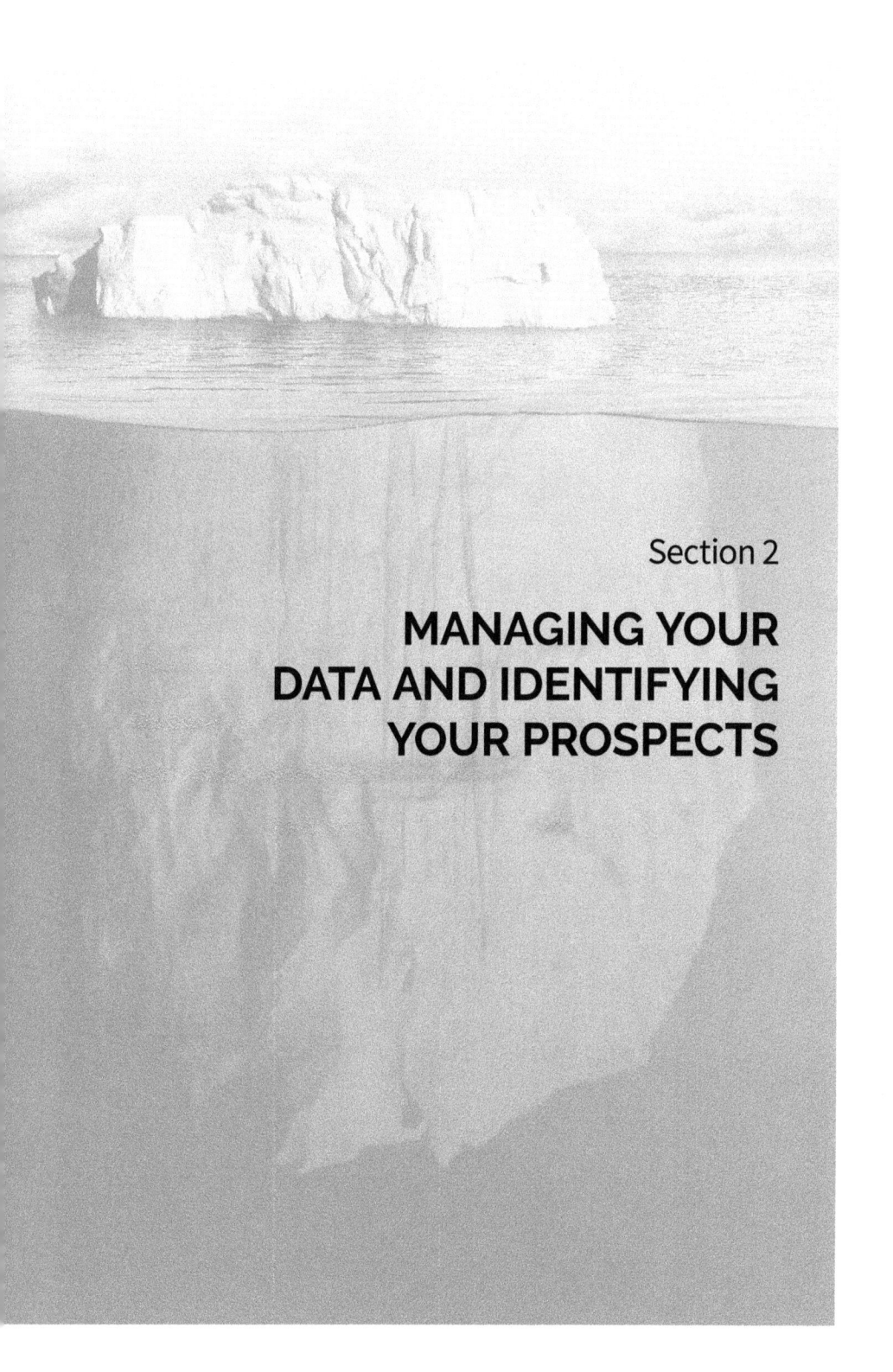

Section 2

MANAGING YOUR DATA AND IDENTIFYING YOUR PROSPECTS

Chapter 4
CONSOLIDATING YOUR DATA

B EFORE you start filling up your pipeline with new prospects, you'll need to think about those prospects that your sales team is already speaking with and those that your marketing automation software is already nurturing. You'll also need to think about your customers. You don't want to cold call companies who your salespeople are already talking to or (even worse) who are already customers. You may still want to call these companies, but you will want to approach these companies in a way that works with rather than against your current relationship. This means that you will need to identify companies that are already prospects, customers or even suppliers so you can either tailor your approach to them or exclude them from your prospecting processes entirely.

This means consolidating your existing data. This is an important part of the process. Too many would-be prospectors leap headfirst into cold calling by purchasing lists of cold prospects. They begin calling these immediately without thinking about whether they are calling companies that are already prospects or customers. For these calls to be remotely effective, there needs to be a different strategy for communicating with these companies, which means we need to identify who is a customer, a supplier, an existing prospect. Until we do this, we can't begin our P2P prospecting campaign. P2P prospecting is absolutely about diving below the waterline and accessing new prospects, but it is also about changing your existing prospect-facing sales and nurturing strategies so that you're delivering the right messages to the right people at the right time.

Remember, you'll be applying your new P2P prospecting strategy to your entire iceberg, which is comprised of the following groups:

- Companies that need your services but have not contacted, or been contacted by, you

- Existing and past prospects who have found you online

- Existing and past prospects your sales team has found through referrals, research, networking, etc.

- Existing customers

- Previous customers (dormant accounts).

If your company is like most organisations, prospect and client data will not be centralised. Different information will be held in different places, in different formats and possibly by different departments as well. Details of your existing and past clients might only be held in your accounting software, whereas your prospect lists are probably shared by Marketing and Sales, often in a Customer Relationship Management application (CRM), in Excel, or in Outlook. Details about prospects that have made online enquiries might only be stored in your website database.

Since you don't want to start cold prospecting to your current and past customers, or to any of the prospects that your sales team are dealing with now or have dealt with in the past—at least not without adjusting your approach considerably—you'll need to exclude from your prospecting lists all those companies that you have already talked to or are still talking to. To do this you'll need a single place to collate all of your prospect and customer records. At this stage, if you don't already have one, you *need* a CRM.

THE IMPORTANCE OF A CRM

A CRM will help you and your sales and marketing teams track all of your prospects as you move them through the various stages of the buying cycle. If you are already using a CRM, you can skip ahead to the next section below. If you are not, you'll need to invest in one *before* you begin prospecting. In today's competitive world, you are putting your sales team at a significant disadvantage if you don't provide them with a good CRM.

A CRM allows your organisation to gather and develop prospect and client records. Anyone in your organisation can make detailed or cursory records of every conversation and piece of correspondence with every prospect, and your sales teams can review these records at any time, often at a glance. Any member of your sales team (regardless of who actually had the conversation) can access and add to these records. If your CRM is a good one, it will also link with your marketing software so that you can seamlessly send information out to prospects as part of your nurturing strategy. It will allow you to track actions and response rates. In short, a good CRM will allow your sales and marketing teams to function as transparent and cooperative units.

There are a number of great systems available, and I'm not going to get into the pros and cons of each here. Some systems are expensive, others less so. Whatever your needs and whatever your budget, choose your CRM with one eye on the horizon. Plan to use the CRM you choose for at least five years. Presuming there are no major hiccups, it is likely you'll be using it much longer than this. It takes time to learn and integrate a new CRM, and once you and your sales teams are used to yours, the considerable time and effort that goes into changing systems will probably make a new CRM an unpopular suggestion. Think ahead and you'll avoid unnecessary friction down the road. Think beyond what you need today to what you will need tomorrow. Pick the CRM that will work the best for you and your specific needs—not the one that's the cheapest.

A key factor in choosing the right system is to select one that can scale without becoming costly. A CRM that allows you to hold up to 5,000 customer records for a small monthly fee may become prohibitively expensive when you have twenty or thirty thousand customer records. Similarly, one that charges a per-user fee might seem fine when you have only two or three users, but these fees can add up to an astronomical amount when your sales teams begin to grow or when you add users in Marketing, Operations and Finance.

GATHER YOUR DATA

Consolidating the data you already have should be your first step. It will show you where the holes in your data are, but also, and more importantly, it will help you ensure that when you order new data from a list broker, you will only be getting new data and not data you already have (this will be covered in substantially more detail in the next chapter).

Consolidating your data is about organisation, but it's also about analysis. With your data in one place, you can start to better understand the contours of your iceberg (first the tip and then the submerged part). Microsoft Excel is a great program to use for this. Most CRMs and accounting packages will export into either a .csv or an Excel format, and regardless of which CRM you choose, they will be able to import your cleaned up, de-duplicated data from Excel, so this is where to begin. Just get all of the customer and prospect information you have from wherever it sits in the organisation into one place by exporting it from your CRM, your accounting software, and so on and gather it all into Excel.

You'll want to make sure your Excel spreadsheet includes all of the following fields, even though you might not have complete information for every company:

- Company name

- Company details
  - Address
    - Street address
    - City
    - State/region
    - Country
    - Postal code
  - Phone numbers
    - Area code
    - Office
  - Size (number of employees)
  - Size (approximate annual revenue)
  - Industry
  - Website
  - Any other pertinent information

- Prospect information
  - Salutation
  - First name
  - Last name
  - Job title

- Prospect contact details
  - Phone numbers
    - Mobile
    - Direct line
  - Email address

- Current status
  - Current customer
    - Last order date
    - Annual spend
  - Previous customer
  - Contacted prospect
    - Products/services of interest
  - Un-contacted prospect
  - Dead prospect (already expressed firm disinterest)
  - Supplier
- Data source.

Remember that each piece of information needs to have its own field (column) in Excel, so, rather than having one field for name (for example, Mr. John Smith), use three separate fields—one for salutation, another for first name, and one more for last name. The list above is by no means exhaustive. You may have additional fields that you want to add. You might want to include a field for the salesperson who is responsible for the account, or one that denotes where the prospect is in the sales cycle, etc. That's fine. Just add them in.

The important thing to remember here is that *every* Excel file that you create, regardless of where the information is coming from (your CRM, accounting software and so on) must have the same field names, and they have to appear in the same order. You are going to be merging these separate files in a moment, and if you don't have the same fields appearing in the same order in every file, your merged data is going to be a mess, with the wrong information appearing in the wrong columns.

For instance if, as is likely, information on the date that a customer last purchased from you is only contained in the data exported from your accounting software, you must include a Last Order Date field in the Excel files that contain the records exported not only from your accounting software, but also in those from your CRM, from Outlook, from your website, and so on, so that you have consistency across all of the files.

Because you will be bringing together data from different sources, I recommend exporting each source to a different Excel file initially. It's just easier than putting everything into multiple worksheets in the same file, and it helps keep the files you are working with a manageable size.

This is also where the Data Source field comes in. When you export data from your accounting software to its own Excel file, add a column called Data Source and put a code (for example, Accounts, or the name of your accounting software) into this field for every record that is in that file. Similarly, when you export the data from your CRM into its own Excel file, indicate the source in the Data Source field with its own code (for example, CRM, or the name of your CRM software). Do this for each source of data that you export so that every Excel file you create has a Data Source field that tells you where this data has come from. When you merge the different Excel files into one master file (see the next section), you'll be able to tell whether records are duplicates from one system, or whether they came from different sources and therefore may contain additional information that was contained in your accounting system, your website, CRM, Outlook, or from somewhere else.

CRITICAL INFORMATION FOR MERGING

Now, before you go off and consolidate all of your client and prospect data into one master file, there is one more step you need to take. You need to review the records in each individual Excel file to make sure that they all contain the *critical* information that will allow you to merge your data successfully. This is the crucial information that those who will use the CRM daily will need. There is, for instance, no point in having records in the CRM that are missing crucial details such as phone number or company name.

The critical information you need to merge your Excel files successfully is:

- **Company name**
- **Area code (phone)**
- **Company phone number**
- **Contact name (salutation, first and last name, plus job title, if possible)**
- Company address 1
- Company address 2
- City
- State
- Postcode
- Country.

The ones in bold are absolutely essential; the rest, less so. Resist the urge not to bother about the non-bolded information, though. The more information you have on each record, the easier it will be to merge the data in your lists and to successfully produce master records. It will also make it much easier to spot duplicate records.

This should be a relatively straightforward process, so it should not take very long to complete. The objective here is to ensure that all *critical information for merging* is present in all of the Excel files, not all information.

Once each record in each file contains all of the critical information, it is time to merge the individual Excel spreadsheets into one master file. And because you have already made sure that all of the individual files contain the same fields (ideally in the same order), you can simply copy the records from one file and paste them into your master file without any data going astray.

CREATING MASTER RECORDS

When you are collating your data, the objective is to create one master record for each company and prospect. When it comes to prospecting, this approach is far superior to more scattered record keeping, with information spread over a number of different systems that are being used by different departments.

With all of your data now in one file, you'll see that you often have multiple records for the same company (one from each source you have imported from). The next step is to start compiling these records into master records—one for each company you'll be prospecting to. Go through the list and review the records, copying all of the information from the duplicate records into a single record in your master Excel file. As you do this, you can delete the old records and any duplicates, but only after you've made sure that they actually are duplicates, and not just two individuals who share the same name. When your sales and marketing teams start making contact with your larger market, they will be using and updating the information in these master records.

Compiling master records is a time-consuming process. Just how time-consuming it will be will depend on how many records you have and how detailed they are. You can assign this task to a member of your staff, or, if you'd rather, you can hire a freelancer (easy enough to find one of these online on sites such as www.upwork.com).

Remember, consolidating all your information is only the beginning of the process. With each new prospect you contact and feed into your pipeline, and with each new client you win you'll be creating new records and adding to existing ones. Consolidating your data will make bringing new contacts into the system a simple process that takes very little time. By making sure that your data is consolidated *before* you start prospecting, you'll be making things easier for you and for your salespeople, who will be working with the new lists that you'll be providing them with. As you'll discover (if you haven't discovered it already), there are virtually no downsides to having fully consolidated data and an up-to-date CRM.

Once you have an Excel document containing all of these master records, the final step is to import this spreadsheet back into your CRM. It's quite possible that you'll need to create new fields in your CRM to accept the new information that you've pulled from your website database and your accounting package, and so on. Again, it's important to make sure that no data gets lost in the shuffle as you move your records and master records from the spreadsheet to the CRM.

WHO YOU GONNA CALL?

The process of data collection and consolidation, especially if you take a hands-on approach, will give you an intimate understanding of your contacts and prospects. Having gone through the data line by line, you can now start separating the wheat from the chaff.

When you start calling, you'll be working with a list (usually a large one) of new prospects. You'll obtain this list from a list broker (see the next chapter), and you'll be seeing many of the names and companies on this list for the first time. Don't let these new prospects carry you away. The last thing you want to do is allow your new prospects to wash your existing ones out of the pipeline. These are some of your hottest prospects, and, though you'll be applying P2P prospecting strategies to contacting and selling to these existing prospects, these strategies will not be identical to the ones you'll be using to approach entirely new prospects. Reach out to old prospects in the same way as you will be reaching out to entirely new ones and you run the risk of alienating them. The strategy is the same, but the message is different.

Separate your existing database contacts into two key segments. In the last section, we covered the Current Status field, and this will come in handy now. Either after you have collated your records or during the process, use the Current Status field to select the contacts that fall into these two categories:

1. Prospects

These are the companies and contacts in your database who are not, and never have been, clients. If they have bought from you at some point, they are either clients or dormant accounts, not prospects. Your prospects have been receiving e-mails and e-marketing materials from you, perhaps for quite some time now. It might be tempting to just write these prospects off (saying, "If they were going to buy, they would have done so already") but remember, they are in your database for a reason. They have expressed a soft or a hard interest at some point. Either they found you online or your sales team found them. If they've expressed an interest of any kind in the past, they have present or future potential.

2. Dormant accounts

These are frequently overlooked, and, when prospected effectively, they can (and often do) prove to be a rich vein of 'new' business. These are the companies that used to buy from you, but haven't done so for a number of years or months (the length of time after which an account becomes dormant will depend on your customers' usual buying cycle). This makes them some of the best leads you have. The reason they are so often overlooked is their sales data has often only been tracked in your accounting software. Since this is not in your CRM, these prospects have slipped off your selling radar. Our data consolidation process has changed this. You know what they purchased and when. They know who you are (as an organisation at least) and what you do. Some of the most difficult prospecting work is already done.

In the calls that Forrest Marketing Group has made to our clients' dormant accounts, we've found that the biggest reason that dormant customers stop using a supplier is that the person who did the buying has left the company. Their replacement, having no relationship with the current supplier, either chooses a supplier with whom they have a relationship or finds somebody new (often somebody who is actively trying to win their business). Without a relationship, it is more difficult to retain a customer. When we call these dormant accounts, it's usually been a couple of years since they moved their business elsewhere. You'd be amazed just how often they are ready to meet with our client and how easy it often is to re-engage them and re-win their business. Even when they took their business elsewhere due to an unresolved or unsatisfactorily resolved issue with our client, merely giving them the chance to vent their frustrations and clear the air has often been enough to re-win their business.

When you start making your prospecting calls (and we'll be looking at how to approach these calls in the next section), you'll want to target both of these prospect categories. You'll also be adding brand new prospects, so you might be starting with quite a large list. Since P2P prospecting is a long-term strategy, you don't have to call everyone immediately. You can start small and ramp up as you start seeing some success with the P2P programme.

When you start calling, it's advisable to begin with the low-hanging fruit—first tapping your dormant accounts and then your hottest prospects. These calls will be the most straightforward ones you'll make. You'll be able to update contact information and, by engaging these prospects in dialogue, you'll be uncovering new opportunities. Because the dormant accounts have bought from you in the past, you know they're qualified (indeed, you probably know their annual spend), so you can focus your efforts on the most worthwhile of these prospects. During these calls, you won't have to spend a great deal of time introducing your organisation or what you're selling. They know the lay of the land; all you'll have to do is tell them about what has improved since they last purchased your product. A word of warning: don't ignore dormant accounts that have a low annual spend. They might be a very large account, but you have only ever had a small "share of wallet".

Calling your dormant accounts and your hottest prospects is a great way to get the prospecting ball rolling. The name of your organisation is already a familiar one. There's already a relationship (even if it's been unattended for some time), and it's simply a matter of, so to speak, rekindling the romance. You'll also be working on your prospecting skills. If you haven't been telephone prospecting for a long time (or ever), these calls and those to other prospects already in your pipeline will help you develop your skills and approach the calls you will soon be making to cold prospects with more confidence, which will make these calls dramatically more successful.

Chapter summary

- You'll be applying your P2P prospecting strategy to your entire market (this includes everything from new prospects to existing clients and those you are already nurturing).

- To consolidate your data, you'll need to invest in a CRM.

- Choose a CRM that is both fit for purpose and scalable (plan to use it for at least five years). Make sure that it can grow as you grow and that the costs associated with it won't become unreasonable as you add more records or users to the system.

- Before importing your data into a CRM, compile a master list using Excel, using as many fields as necessary to ensure that no piece of important information gets lost in the shuffle.

- P2P prospecting will make the most of the lists you'll be purchasing, but it will also change the way you approach your existing prospects (those already in your pipeline) and dormant accounts (former clients who can be brought back into the fold).

- Your existing prospects and dormant accounts are some of your best prospects, so they will be a great place to start when you adopt P2P prospecting. These calls will be the easiest ones you'll make, so they'll help your sales team build confidence and enthusiasm—both of which they'll need for the work ahead.

Chapter 5

BUILDING A NEW LIST

NOW that you've consolidated your data, it's time to start looking below the waterline. The companies you've been targeting up to this point are only the tip of your iceberg. It's time to get a clearer picture of the entirety of your potential market. For many people, even thinking about identifying their potential market is daunting. Which companies are they? What or who are they using now? Where are they? How do I find them? All of these questions and more pile one upon the other until the task starts to take on what feels like gargantuan proportions. At this point, we usually put off the task for a later date or give it up entirely, making do with our existing understanding of our potential market.

By doing this, though, we are doing our sales teams a dramatic disservice. Most sales teams are performing at around half of their potential, simply because they are only selling to the tip of the iceberg. When you dip below the waterline, you'll be bringing your salespeople with you, and this will change not only the way they operate but also their ability to perform well beyond your expectations.

Defining your market is, I assure you, not as daunting a task as you might think. Let's get started by taking another look at your iceberg:

- The tip is made up of those prospects who are searching right now for what you sell. They are the ones scouring the Internet for solutions (solutions that you—and your competitors—can provide). By and large, your sales team isn't finding these prospects; rather, these prospects are finding you, usually as a result of online research. They are in your pipeline and are therefore receiving e-marketing messages and, for those at the very tip of the iceberg, they are actually opening them. They are the 1.9% (those who are not only receiving marketing messages but opening them and clicking through). The tip of your iceberg also includes your dormant accounts that might be brought back into the fold.

- Below the waterline are the prospects who aren't actively searching for what you sell. You may have brushed up against them in some of your broader digital marketing campaigns, but not enough for them to register on your radar. The vast majority of the iceberg beneath the surface is comprised of prospects who are not in your database yet. They probably don't know that you can help them resolve a specific issue they've been ignoring or living with—indeed, they might not even know you exist. Your salespeople aren't talking to them because they have remained, thus far, submerged. They form a huge but unaddressed portion of your potential market. It's time to change that.

Later on, we're going to discuss how to approach the tip of your iceberg. These are your best prospects, and nothing that we'll be discussing in the next section will try to convince you otherwise. For now, though, we want to put on our diving mask and take a look beneath the waterline. We'll want to bring an oxygen tank while we're at it, because we're going to be down there for a while. Once we see what's hiding beneath the waterline, we'll be spending just as much time talking to these new prospects as old ones. We'll be building strong and meaningful relationship with these prospects, but before we do that, we need to know who they are.

Your competitors probably don't know who these prospects are, and if by chance they do, it's highly unlikely that they're approaching them in the way that you soon will be. They're probably just sending them automated marketing messages, and probably without much success. We're going to start approaching these prospects and engaging them in person-to-person conversations, and this is something your competitors almost certainly aren't doing.

Before we start prospecting, though, you'll need to do the difficult work of defining your market. This is going to give you a more accurate picture—one that includes the huge numbers of submerged prospects in your market. With this picture you'll build a sustainable and predictable sales pipeline—one that will make you the envy of your competitors. This will require no mean amount of hard work, but in the words of Lao Tzu, *"A journey of a thousand miles begins with a single step."*

Too often, good projects with good ideas behind them die before they even get started. They die because nobody took that crucial and difficult first step, and defining your market is the first step of any prospecting campaign worth its salt. Most prospecting efforts come undone simply because those who attempt them simply don't take the time to define their market at all, or they don't do it thoroughly enough. As a result, when their sales team starts prospecting, they waste their time calling too many companies who have no use for their products or services. Approach this stage without due care, and you and your team will quickly lose any motivation or enthusiasm you might have had for prospecting. Sales teams using poor prospecting lists often terminate their campaigns prematurely, convinced that prospecting just doesn't work. Prepare your lists carefully, though, and early results will produce enthusiasm, which spreads through sales teams like wildfire.

OUR FIRST GLIMPSE OF THE ICEBERG

According to the Australian Bureau of Statistics, there were roughly 2.2 million businesses in Australia in 2016, with the number growing by around 1% per year. However, they also report that 61% of the registered businesses have no staff at all. When I ask my clients how many companies they think might be suitable prospects for their business, most of them just shrug their shoulders. Fortunately, there is a straightforward way to find this out. There are companies that own and manage databases of organisations. These are the list brokers. They own databases of businesses in every conceivable market, and, for a reasonable fee, they will sell you a list of these prospects. How you approach these list brokers will determine the quality of what they can and will provide for you, so read the information in this section carefully.

There are several very good list brokers. Each has its own range of accurate and up-to-date databases prepared according to a number of different criteria. Some are very good for targeting large organisations, others for targeting small and medium-size ones. Some provide information on companies' IT infrastructure, others have data on their creditworthiness. These list brokers can provide you with an estimate of the number of companies in your target market and then, for a fee (probably less than you think), they can provide you with a list of these companies. The long-term goal is to have a list of potential prospects that is as large as you can manage. These are the people you'll be feeding into your P2P prospecting pipeline, and you'll be staying in touch with them through their buying journey.

List brokers can only ever be as good as you tell them to be (that is, the list you ask for is the list you get). The more specific and targeted your criteria are, the better the results you can expect. You can control the quality of companies you are funnelling into your sales pipeline by controlling the criteria by which you ask the list broker to filter their databases. Let's take a look at how to do this. We are going to think about our target market using four criteria at this stage:

1. Geographic location – Where are your prospects located?

2. Industry – What industries are your prospects in?

3. Size – What size of company is your ideal prospect?

4. Office type – Head office, only office or all office types?

Let's take a look at each of these in more detail.

1. Geographic location

This may sound obvious, but it's not something you should take for granted. Ask yourself where your ideal customers are located. Don't ask yourself where they are; rather, ask where they could or should be. Just because the majority of your clients are, for example, based in your immediate vicinity, doesn't mean you should only be looking next door—especially not when widening your search will substantially increase the size of your potential market, and will, in turn, increase (often dramatically) the number of companies that your list broker will be able to provide.

You may decide to prospect only in locations where you have a sales team, but remember that you may be eliminating a lot of possible clients if you do this. Let's face it, if you found a great prospect who was based in a location that you or one of your salespeople had to travel to, would you find a way to make that meeting happen? Sure you would, so don't cast a small net unless you absolutely have to. For your first cut, you'll want to cast your net wide enough to catch all of your potential prospects.

2. Industry

Just as with questions about location, being too precious about the industry or industries you want to target will significantly limit the number of qualified prospects your list broker can give you. The standard and most precise way of describing and classifying industry segments in Australia and New Zealand is known as the Australia and New Zealand Standard Industrial Classification (ANZSIC) system. ANZSIC is a four-level hierarchical system of classification based on business activity. Moving from the broadest to the finest categories, there are Divisions, Subdivisions, Groups and Classes. Here's an example of what this might look like if you're trying to locate companies with meat processing as their primary business activity.

Division	C	Manufacturing
Subdivision	11	Food and Product Manufacturing
Group	111	Meat and Meat Product Manufacturing
Class	1111	Meat Processing

You can download a copy of the ANZSIC codes from the following link: http://www.impactlists.com.au/List-Tools.aspx.

Choose the 2006 ANZSIC codes, which are listed under Tools.

To begin with just select the Divisions that are relevant to you. This is quick as there are only 19 of these. It should be fairly easy to eliminate the ones that you are not interested in. Remember, it's always easier to start with all of them and, after some consideration, eliminate one industry at a time than it is to work the other way around. Keeping your criteria as broad as possible means you'll be starting with a much larger list. Let's say, for instance, that you were to select companies in Division F (Wholesale). If you were to add Division G (Retail), you would be increasing your list size by almost 94,000 companies. Adding or removing a single criterion might double or halve the size of your iceberg, so choose carefully.

Once you've selected the Divisions you're interested in, you want to start breaking these down further by Class. There are 506 of these in total, so you can get quite detailed and niched, but you'll only be considering the ones that fall in the Divisions you have already selected.

3. Size

You'll want to think about what size of company you're currently dealing with and what size of company you'd like to deal with as your company grows. Your ideal prospects are going to be companies of a specific size, or companies that fall within a certain desirable size range. You want to avoid getting a list that contains companies that are either far too small or far too big to be good clients for you.

There are two ways to define company size: number of staff and annual turnover. Which one is right for you will depend largely on what you sell. For example, if you provide a user-based solution such as software for architectural companies, the number of staff in the organisation is a good indicator of how big a customer that company will be, so you will want your list to contain companies that are in a specific size range based on the number of staff in the organisation. The same is true if you provide an outsourced payroll solution, where a good client would, again, be easily defined by the number of staff they have. However, if you provide logistics and supply chain management to companies that export goods overseas, company turnover is going to provide a much better indicator of how big an account a company is likely to be.

A word of caution: if you are selecting based on annual turnover, the information most list brokers will provide will almost certainly be based on estimates (using industry averages). As with any estimates, they might be on the money or they might miss the mark by a considerable margin. This doesn't mean that turnover is a poor selection criteria, just that you should bear the relative inaccuracy of these estimates in mind.

There is another way to estimate annual turnover, which is pretty accurate for smaller businesses. There is often a dependable correlation between the number of staff that a company employs and that company's annual revenue. The correlation may not be exact, but it is a helpful guideline when you're compiling a list of SMEs. The rule of thumb to apply here is as follows: every full-time staff member is equivalent to $120,000 in annual revenue. If, for example, you want to target companies with a turnover of $3 to $10 million, you could do this by selecting companies that employ between 25 and 80 people. The larger companies grow, however, the less reliable this formula will become.

Setting the right parameters around the size of company you want to work with is very important. Often, when I am helping clients decide what size of company they want to target, they say, "We sell to any size of company", or "We have clients who are one-man companies, as well as some that are huge corporates". Though it is wise to cast a wide net, all companies have a 'sweet spot', and this never includes companies of every conceivable size. Sure, you *can* sell to everybody, but as company size decreases, so too does its budget. Include too many small companies and you'll probably end up wasting the time of your sales team on meetings with companies that either can't afford your solution or will only ever become small accounts—and that's not where you want your sales team to focus their efforts.

When selecting the size of company that you want to include on your prospecting list, make sure that the smallest companies you select really will represent good prospects for you. There are far more small companies than there are large ones, so you can expect that when you get your list from your list broker, you will find more companies at the smaller end of your size range. Plotted on a graph, your list will almost certainly be pear shaped. Be careful with your criteria. If the companies on your list aren't near or right in the middle of your sweet spot, you'll soon be dealing with a frustrated sales team, or you'll be wondering why your team is only bringing in very small accounts.

4. Office type

Depending on what you're selling, office type may make all the difference to the relevance of the records contained on your list, or it may make no difference at all. If you ask them to, list brokers can narrow down their lists to include only head offices or organisations with only one office. Or they can provide lists that include all branch offices. If you sell to retail businesses, you'll want to decide whether your market is every branch of a retail company or just its head office. If you sell to banks, are your prospects going to be the individual branches or the head office? If you include branch offices in your search criteria when your target market is actually only the head office, your search results could be grossly overinflated. Once again, you'll be wasting your sales team's time (and testing their patience).

Target Market Definition for Forrest Marketing Group

Here is a sample profile that shows the search criteria I've used when requesting lists for my company's prospecting. You'll notice that I keep it quite broad. When I first submitted search criteria to my list broker, I was quite selective and was underwhelmed with the number of matches they returned with. Each time I broadened my criteria, my iceberg grew considerably, and today, some of my best clients are those who I would have missed had I not broadened my initial criteria.

Our ideal clients are Australian companies with a turnover of $4 million or more. We also need our prospects to have a sales team selling a product or service with a sales value of $15,000 or more. While we have worked (and will continue to work) with companies that do not adhere to these criteria, these are not *ideal clients;* we try not to spend too much of our time trying to win clients that either don't (or just barely) meet what we have defined as our minimum requirements. We know that prospecting is best approached as a long-term process. The best results are always the product of a consistently run, year-round campaign. We therefore seek out clients who are likely to have a budget of $60,000 or more that they can spend on sales campaigns, which is what they would spend with us for a consistent prospecting programme.

Ideal Client Profile	Selection Criteria for List Broker	Specific Criteria Required
Should be located anywhere in Australia	Geographic area	Any location, Australia-wide
Should sell products or services to other businesses (B2B)	Industries	Agriculture, Mining, Manufacturing, Electricity, Gas, Water and Waste Services, Construction, Wholesale, Transport, Postal and Warehousing, Information Media and Telecommunications, Financial and Insurance Services, Professional, Scientific and Technical Services, Administrative and Support Services, Other Services.
Company annual turnover should be min. $4 million/year	Annual Turnover	$4 million+
Should have a sales team	Number of Staff	40 staff+
Their decision maker (DM) will probably be based at Head Office	Office Type	Head or Only Office

CHOOSING A LIST BROKER

Now that you have your target market defined, it's time to start talking to list brokers. Send them your target market definition and ask them to give you a count of the records that match your selection criteria. You may find that one list broker has many more (or many fewer) records than another. Choose the list broker with the largest number of records that match your criteria (that is, the one that gives you the largest iceberg to work with). The size of the list tells you how large your target market is and how many companies you can start prospecting to. If you've been broad enough with your criteria, this list should introduce you to quite a few new target organisations that have been, thus far, below the waterline. You can also ask your list broker to break their list down further according to state or city, which will help you further understand the geographical contours of your market and help you to decide where to start your prospecting calls.

Getting a count of records is usually a free service, so if a list broker asks for a fee to provide a count, it might be wise to start looking elsewhere. While most list brokers will be obliging when you ask them for a preliminary records count, don't ask them to jump through too many hoops at this stage. Once you've decided on a list broker, you can start massaging the lists in a variety of ways, but don't expect list brokers to show you their hand before there's money in the pot. Giving them the list criteria that you developed earlier is fine, as is asking them to give you a breakdown by either location (state), industry or company size. However, during these preliminary stages, repeatedly going back for more and more details, asking for a breakdown by postcode or asking for complex breakdowns (the number of companies in one industry with 10-50 staff versus the number in another industry with 50-100 staff) is probably going to push the friendship too far. So long as you provide them with clear search criteria, you can expect the list broker to come back to you with a list count within one or two days at most.

Once you've decided which list broker you'll be working with, don't be shy about asking them for advice. Reputable list brokers know their products very well. They'll be able to guide you to the best list for your needs. If they provide you with a number of different options, ask them which list they think would be the best fit for your organisation and for your target market. It's unlikely that they'll lead you astray.

There are a number of Australian list brokers to choose from, all of them quite easy to locate online. Some of them are, as you'd expect, better than others. Here are some of the list brokers that we use regularly. The difference between lists from different list brokers is often striking, so I suggest that you talk to at least two list brokers before making a decision.

- **Dataphoria (Sydney) – www.dataphoria.com.au**

  Dataphoria is a broker for many different lists. They tend to produce the best results for those who are attempting to target a very narrow or otherwise difficult market. Though they provide very good straightforward lists, they claim to love the challenge of filling unusual requests.

- **Dun & Bradstreet (Melbourne) – www.dnb.com.au**

  Dun & Bradstreet has a comprehensive database and is, unlike some other providers, able to provide the annual turnover for many of the companies they keep records on. Note that a lot of this annual turnover data is modelled. Their estimates are not entirely reliable, but if turnover is an important criterion for you, this might be a good place to start (albeit with a degree of caution). They also collect credit data on companies, which can be extremely useful if risk and debt management are important factors for you.

- **Impact Lists (Melbourne) – www.impactlists.com.au**

  Like Dataphoria, Impact is a broker for many different lists, and also has its own list, Reach DM, making it a good one-stop shop for lists.

- **IncNet (Sydney) – www.incnet.com.au**

  IncNet cover the top 55,000 businesses in Australia, so it is a good place to start if you want to target the top end of town. They have also recently taken over a database called MarketBase, which focuses on the top 9,000 companies in Australia and New Zealand. This list is rich in C-suite contacts and contains very detailed IT infrastructure information.

- **Prospect Shop (Sydney) – www.prospectshop.com.au**

  Now owned by Veda, another company that collects credit, risk and debt management information, the Prospect Shop is a broker of many lists, similar to Impact Lists and Dataphoria.

An additional service that some list brokers provide is list profiling. This involves taking a subset of your database (your best customers, for instance), profiling these companies, and then identifying other companies that match or nearly match these profiles. This can be a very powerful way to home in on great below-the-waterline prospects—particularly when you're trying to get a clear look at hard-to-define markets. You will probably need to give the list broker a few hundred companies to match against, but some brokers can do more with less. Ask them about what list profiling services they offer, and they'll tell you exactly what they need.

If the results you get from your list broker are less than what you'd hoped for, the problem might not be with the list provider—it might be with your criteria. So if you are struggling to identify your market with a list broker, you may want to look at other options. For instance, you can use LinkedIn in conjunction with list profiling to help zero in on companies or contacts below the waterline.

Here's how we did this for one of our clients: the client wanted to target the Head of IT in companies with an internal call centre, but searches for companies that fit that profile only turned up companies like mine (that is, dedicated call centres). Excluded were the banks, utility providers, retailers, finance and insurance companies, all of which have call centres. We went on LinkedIn and searched by job title (using Call Centre Manager and other similar titles as a guide). We built a list of companies that had an employee that matched that job title and then returned to the list broker and got them to give us the contact details for the Head of IT in each of these companies. In the end we ended up getting a list even larger than we had hoped for.

Once your list broker comes back to you with a records count, you'll have (perhaps for the first time) an idea of how big your iceberg actually is. You might be looking at thousands of potential prospects. It's usually at this stage that people start to realise that they're really on to something.

HOW BIG DOES MY LIST NEED TO BE?

I said earlier that your initial list count should be on the larger side because you want to know how big your market actually is. However, you don't want to get carried away when ordering your first list. When you buy your list, you'll want to buy only enough records to last you around three months. If you're purchasing your first list intending to prospect with it for much longer than three months, the data will start to degrade noticeably. Some people think it is a good idea to make their first list one with enough records on it to last them a full year. It's better by far to start small, looking three to four months ahead. People change jobs every two to three years, which means that, if you have a list big enough to last you a full year, one-third to half of the people on your list will no longer be the contact person at the company by the time you get around to calling them. Also, what if you make a mistake in the records you have ordered? If your list turns out to be unusable, it will be much less painful to discard a small list than a really large one

After your first three months of prospecting, you'll have a much better understanding of your iceberg and its contours, but you'll also know quite a bit more about precisely what companies to target to be successful. Whenever appropriate, modify your selection criteria based on feedback from your sales team. This feedback might lead you toward entirely new markets; when you pivot in this way, once again, you'll be glad you didn't drop a bundle on a large list.

The exact number of company records that you need for your initial prospecting list will depend on how many sales staff will be making the prospecting calls. Each member of my team makes between 15 and 22 phone calls per hour, and you should expect about the same from your own prospectors. Because people are often in meetings, on the phone, or away from their desks when called, you'll find that 15-22 calls per hour usually translates to conversations with 4-7 contacts with decision makers per hour, which is around a four to one call to contact ratio. Those who are not reached on the first try are earmarked for a later call back.

AN ILLUSTRATIVE EXAMPLE

Let's say that two members of your sales team are going to start prospecting. Let's also say that you decide on a goal of each team member speaking to 20 new prospects per week (with two prospectors, they'll be speaking with a total of 40 prospects per week between them). If you do this for three months (13 weeks), here is what you'll need to allow:

- Each salesperson will need to make around 80 prospecting calls per week to reach 20 new prospects. That's 160 calls in total each week.

- After 13 weeks, each salesperson will have reached 260 prospects, or 520 in total. Remember that reaching a prospect means a conversation with the appropriate decision maker, not just a conversation with whoever answers the phone.

This does not mean that your list should have 520 records for 13 weeks of prospecting. You need quite a bit of a buffer, otherwise your salespeople will start running out of prospects well before they get to the end of the three months. Without this buffer, your prospectors will end up chasing a shrinking number of prospects. Contacts still to be called will become increasingly hard to come by as your prospecting campaign enters its second month. In the third month your prospectors will be calling a list of people who, for whatever reason, are difficult if not impossible to get on the phone. At this point your prospectors will not be making anywhere near their 20 calls an hour, or speaking with many prospects.

To avoid this, I use a rule of thumb: order additional records, equivalent to two weeks' worth of phone calls. So, in this case, where your prospectors are making 160 phone calls per week between them, you'll need to order an additional 320 records. This should be added to the total number of prospects that your prospectors will *speak* to over the three-month period (520). The total number of records you should order in this example is therefore 840. You don't need to be too precise, so you can merely ask your list broker to provide you with somewhere between 800 and 900 records.

This will ensure that your salespeople or prospectors won't be scraping the bottom of the barrel to find people to call at the end of the three months. While prospecting off a fresh list can be a pleasant experience, using a list that has been overcalled is gruelling work.

As we move forward, it's important to remember that even the best prospectors are prone to burnout and sagging enthusiasm. You can combat this by making sure to refresh the pipeline regularly with new prospects. Prospecting is not a set-it-and-forget-it strategy. A big part of P2P prospecting success is traced to the quality of the raw materials you feed it—meaning the quality of the list you provide to your prospectors. P2P prospecting, as I always say, can produce incredible results, but only if it's diligently and consistently applied over the long term, and only if you're ensuring that new contacts are constantly being fed into the prospecting pipeline. Once you've called through your first list, be sure to go back to the list broker (or try a different one) for the next batch of prospects.

Chapter summary

- Before you start calling, you'll need a list of new prospects to call.

- By approaching list brokers with the right criteria, you'll be getting below the waterline, seeing for the first time the actual size of your iceberg.

- Select your list broker carefully. Don't purchase a list until you're quite sure that you're getting value for your money.

- To define your market, apply the following four criteria:

  1. Geographic location
  2. Industry
  3. Size
  4. Office type.

- You can use the ANZSIC system to get the right industry selections.

- Once you've provided them with search criteria, good list brokers will provide you with a list count (usually within a few days). Choose the list broker with the largest list that fits your criteria.

- Don't be shy about asking list brokers for advice. Talk to them about your ideal customers. They'll guide you to the list that is best suited to your needs.

- If your list broker offers it as a service, use list profiling to find a list of prospects that match your current or ideal customers.

- When purchasing your first list, do so planning for no more than 3-4 months of prospecting.

- A successful P2P prospecting strategy is one that regularly feeds fresh prospects into the prospecting pipeline, so plan to purchase new prospecting lists at regular intervals.

Chapter 6
PREPARING FOR FIRST CONTACT

S O now you've got a whizz-bang new list in your hands. You might be tempted (and plenty of people have fallen into this trap) to just feed that list into your existing sales and marketing machine. You've been using these techniques for years with limited success, so there's nothing to suggest that a replenished pipeline without a change in approach will produce anything other than what you've already been getting. You're reading this book, so it's safe to assume you want to lift your sales performance. To do that, we need to take the next step. You need to pick up that phone and start dialling.

You've dipped below the waterline. You know what your iceberg looks like, you know who you're going to call, now it's just a matter of reaching out and touching that part of your market that has been (before now) submerged and hidden from view. This can't be done in any meaningful way without a conversation—not a one-way sales pitch but a two-way dialogue, one that finds out who these prospects are and what their needs and issues are.

We've learned to rely on digital marketing so heavily that many of us have lost touch with the delicate art of one-to-one prospecting. P2P prospecting takes time and effort, and, if it's an approach you haven't used before, even the thought of picking up the phone might send shivers down your spine, or that of your sales team. We'll be starting slowly, and we'll discuss some of the ways you can make each call count in the next section, but before we get to the content of the calls, I need to convince you that your sales team needs to pick up the phone in the first place. This is, I assure you, the largest barrier. Once you've pushed through it and started dialling, you'll soon see the value of the conversation. You'll wonder why you haven't started doing this earlier.

The conversation is what puts you in pole position. It's not about producing immediate sales (though it does this as well). P2P prospecting puts you in touch with people who are ready to buy, as well as prospects who don't yet have an immediate, pressing need. Here, you will be building relationships and uncovering those places where the prospect's shoes rub or pinch. They have been living with their problems, possibly for quite some time, but perhaps they assume that rubbing and pinching is just what shoes do. You're going to use the conversation to plant an idea in their head—the idea that you can offer them a better-fitting shoe.

We're going to be using conversations to build relationships, and these relationships are going to translate to a dramatic increase in sales. If you've compiled your lists carefully, the prospects you talk to are going to buy either what you're selling or something very similar to it at some point. They might be below the waterline for you, but this doesn't guarantee that your competitors haven't spotted them already. Even if they're receiving marketing messages from your competitors, they might not be talking to them in any meaningful way. By starting a dialogue with them, you immediately move to the front of the prospect's mind. The quality of engagement is higher, and so is the likelihood that, when they're ready to purchase, it will be from you—perhaps this will be tomorrow, perhaps it will be later this year, but the end result will be the same: a sale.

You'll also be nurturing these prospects with emails and other digital marketing messages, but these will be reinforcing a dialogue-grounded relationship. They're hearing your voice almost as often as they're seeing your name in their inbox. You'll be braiding your P2P prospecting and your digital marketing campaigns together, and this will make your sales process much more effective.

REMOVING THE STIGMA SURROUNDING TELEPHONE PROSPECTING

There's a stigma attached to cold calling. Almost nobody claims to enjoy doing it, and fewer people wax poetic about the joys of receiving "telemarketing" calls. Today's salespeople feel as though telephone prospecting is somehow beneath their status. It is, they say, old fashioned, and what's worse, it doesn't work. Nobody, they say, wants to pick up the phone to find a salesperson on the other end of the line.

Critics of telephone prospecting even question how telephone prospecting might affect a company's brand. They worry that they will be using an aggressive approach, which will damage their brand and make it harder, not easier, to find and win new customers. Talk like this has scared the bejeezus out of those who might have otherwise considered telephone prospecting as a sales strategy. But the stigma surrounding telephone prospecting is the product of a time when the market was positively saturated with it and pushy sales calls were all the rage. Times have changed. P2P prospecting means having a conversation, not making a one-way, pushy sales call. You can now approach telephone prospecting with an open mind, and when you do you'll see that it works, and it works in ways that today's other marketing and sales campaigns don't (and indeed can't) work.

The proof is in the pudding. My company, Forrest Marketing Group, has been running since 2006, and we have around 80 agents working the phones at any given time. Every week, these agents make thousands of cold calls and set hundreds of appointments for our clients' sales teams. The leads we have developed for our clients (the vast majority of them from prospects who were well below the waterline) have turned into hundreds of millions of dollars in new business. I see sales prospecting every day, and I can say—with certainty—that cold calling works, and it works very well. Why does it work so well? For two reasons: first, it creates a relationship that e-marketing campaigns only mimic; second, almost nobody is doing it.

Because so few people are doing it, there's an assumption that telephone prospecting doesn't work, or that it is dead. It's not dead, it's just living under an assumed name: the discovery call. Professional prospectors are using discovery calls every day to engage with prospects and uncover their needs. These calls share all of the features of cold calls, but they are handled so professionally that prospects don't feel as though they're being cold called. They feel as though they are being discovered.

It is true: the type of cold calling that gave prospectors a bad name in the '80s and '90s is no longer an effective sales strategy. These are the poorly structured sales calls—the ones with pushy salespeople who try, almost always unsuccessfully, to foist their product or service on you without letting you get a word in edgewise. This is what gave telemarketing its bad name. The pushy telemarketer isn't yet extinct, though they should be. However, it's not the sales call itself that's the problem—it's the approach.

If you asked your sales team to call a list of prospects, would you consider their calls to be telemarketing calls? Probably not. Imagine that you are sitting in your office and the phone rings. It's the sales rep from a well-known CRM provider. He's calling to ask you about which CRM you are using, how it is working for you and what your issues are. Would you consider that to be a telemarketing call? Again, probably not. You'd think of it as a sales call, a sales prospecting call, perhaps, but it's unlikely that you'd think that you had just received a telemarketing call—unless, that is, the salesperson took a pushy, take-no-prisoners approach. The approach I'll be advocating in the next section is built upon a conversational style, one that is never one-sided or pushy. When it's done correctly, the prospect won't feel as though they've been cold called.

Now you could argue, and I'm sure someone will, that there are better ways to reach prospects than to call them up out of the blue, but experience has taught me that calling is the best way to reach and engage with prospects. Anyone who says that e-marketing and email campaigns are better than telephone prospecting has a lot of explaining to do (particularly when it comes to the abysmal open and click through rates).

Telephone prospecting has success rates that e-marketing campaigns can only dream of. In the prospecting calls that we make for our clients, we set, on average, an appointment with one in every 17 decision-makers that we speak to (a conversion rate of around 6%). Remember that these are prospects who, by and large, are not looking for our clients' services when we call. Our call has, for the first time, formed a bridge between a seller and a purchaser; our call has also uncovered an opportunity and qualified the prospect's need.

Roughly 1 in 17 of the prospects we talk to are ready to meet today. About 50% of the remaining 16 prospects (the ones who we don't immediately book an appointment with) are valid and qualified prospects. They don't have an immediate need, but they do have a future need. They are added to the client's sales funnel and followed up at the appropriate time. Even a single prospector working part-time in a dedicated way for a year will add between 2,000 and 3,500 of these future prospects into the sales pipeline. Let's be really, really conservative and say you only convert 2% of these into sales in the first year. That's still 40-70 new clients, and that's on top of the prospects you are meeting who have an immediate need, and on top of the sales you're already making. Most companies would kill for this sort of boost to their sales pipeline. No matter how exceptionally well managed your online marketing campaigns are, it's highly unlikely they're doing for you what even a single prospector can.

It may be easier just to send out an email to thousands of potential customers and wait for the responses to come pouring back in, but today's customers are less and less likely to respond to these messages; they need that personal contact, and it's cold calling that can and does provide it. Prospecting calls need to be thought of as an essential step in the sales process. They are the best way to reach a large number of prospects in a short amount of time, and they make this contact meaningful. Your offer can be personalised based on each prospect's particular needs or issues, making it far more enticing. That's selling, and it's selling to your entire market, both above and below the waterline.

COMMON OBJECTIONS (TO COLD CALLING)

When you decide to make P2P prospecting a part of your sales strategy, a few objections are bound to come up. Some of these will come from the management team, others from the sales team. Most will reflect some of the misconceptions surrounding telephone prospecting. Some of these objections will point to a deeper issue: fear. You'll want to be armed with ways to address these objections and put people's minds (and fears) at rest. Let's look at a few of the more common objections in detail:

1. **Cold calling will damage our brand.**

   This objection fails to see the difference between the kind of telephone prospecting we'll be describing in the next section and the kind of pushy telemarketing that dominated the sales landscape in the '80s and '90s. It's never bad for your brand when your sales team is talking with (not *at*) potential prospects about what your products or services could do for them. A well-structured prospecting call guided by a personable and polite sales representative enhances your reputation and brand. It keeps your market informed and, prospect by prospect, it builds relationships. Of course it is *possible* for prospecting calls to damage your brand, but only when it's the wrong kind of conversation and the wrong kind of salesperson. You run the same amount of risk when you give your salespeople the freedom to email or meet with clients, and you do that every day. Even if you have salespeople who aren't comfortable with telephone prospecting, you'll be providing them with straightforward guidance that will ensure they're having the right, on-message conversations.

2. **Sales teams just don't have the time to spend on the phone.**

   Quite the contrary, your salespeople don't have the time *not* to be on the phone. Without prospecting, they aren't making nearly as many sales as they could be. They're relying on online enquiries and other leads generated by Marketing, and there aren't nearly as many of these enquiries as there used to be. While they don't need to spend all day, every day on the phone, they do need to make P2P prospecting a significant part of their approach to the market.

   If your sales team really is too busy nurturing and selling to existing leads to handle extra duties, or if you are concerned about paying high-cost sales staff to make their own prospecting calls, you can outsource the process either in part or entirely to a reliable company. If you do outsource the process, your sales team should be doing at least some of their own prospecting. They could be using the techniques that are outlined in the next chapters of this book to start meaningful conversations with companies and prospects they have met at networking events, conferences, expos, or elsewhere. They know their products and how to sell them better than anyone, so they are best placed to uncover the needs of prospects and to handle their questions and objections.

3. **Cold calling won't work for my business/products/services.**

   This is more often an excuse than it is a reality, though it may be true in a few isolated cases. For instance, if your niche or target market is not one that can be defined through search criteria, finding companies to prospect to can be extremely difficult. Some creative thinking might solve this, though. Take the example of a wedding photographer: if the photographer only thinks about their target market as couples preparing for a march down the aisle, cold calling won't be very effective (imagine calling hundreds or perhaps thousands of people and asking them if they are getting married soon). If, however, the photographer changed their target market to wedding planners and wedding venues (the people who *connect* them to their end-customers), prospecting could now prove extremely effective. If you're convinced that cold calling won't work for you, you might be right, but you might be thinking too narrowly about your target market.

   If what you're selling is virtually indistinguishable from what your competitors offer (common for lawyers, accountants, and organisations that offer managed IT support for instance), sales prospecting may not work for you, unless you can present the prospect with a compelling reason to meet. But remember, whether you believe sales prospecting will or won't work for you, you will be right. With some creative thinking, you can usually come up with an approach that will work (we'll talk about this again later). In my experience, there is almost always something that you can do, and something is always better than nothing.

4. **My sales team will never go for cold calling.**

It's true; most salespeople will do just about anything to get out of making sales prospecting calls. In my experience, if you ask a salesperson to choose whether they would rather cold call or dive headfirst into a freezing lake, they will always choose the lake. Don't give them the option. By creating the right environment, setting the right expectations, and by providing the right training, motivation and management, you can turn a must-do into an enjoy-to-do. If you can't convince them, you can always outsource your prospecting. We'll take a closer look at outsourcing options later in this book.

Overcoming these objections might be difficult at first. There is almost bound to be friction when changing approaches (especially when those who are using these approaches have grown comfortable with the status quo). After a few months, though, you (and they) will be starting to reap what you've sown. The increased pipeline flow and efficiency will make the early friction a thing of the past.

In the next section, I'll be giving you the tools and approaches you'll need to make prospecting work for you. One final piece of advice before we get started: don't get lured into the trap of doing nothing. Making prospecting a core task—and doing so in sustainable ways—is one of those things that, as Jeff Olson says in his book, *The Slight Edge,* is "easy to do … and just as easy not to do." Sure it's easy to just let your online marketing campaigns continue to bring trickles of customers through your doors, but it's not much harder to dive below the waterline and start speaking with potential customers directly rather than waiting for them to come to you. The biggest difference isn't the effort; it's merely the will. Be willing to do what others won't and you'll enjoy the success that's out of reach to those who are running exclusively with the digital herd.

Chapter summary

- Resist the urge to feed your new list into your existing digital marketing pipeline.

- A new list won't plug the holes in your leaky pipeline. The time and money you've invested in the process up to this point will be wasted if you're not nurturing the prospects in your pipeline effectively.

- The largest barrier you'll encounter in the process is the one that stands between you or your sales teams and the first calls you'll be making or having them make. Once you've broken through this barrier, you'll find things become progressively easier.

- P2P prospecting is about building relationships, and these relationships translate to more sales.

- Braiding P2P prospecting and your ongoing digital marketing campaigns will lead to a much more efficient and effective sales process.

- If you feel anxious about cold calling as a strategy, it's probably because you remember a time when the market was saturated with pushy cold callers. Times have changed, and the market is now more receptive to telephone prospecting (so long as the approach is appropriate).

- Cold calling works for two reasons:

  a. It creates a relationship between the customer and the seller that digital marketing campaigns can only mimic.
  b. Nobody else (or next to nobody) is doing it.

- Anybody who says that e-marketing is more effective than telephone prospecting has probably never tried the latter. When done right, P2P prospecting has a success rate that e-marketing campaigns can only dream of.

- When you decide to make P2P prospecting a part of your sales strategy, you'll almost certainly encounter some resistance from your sales staff. Much of this resistance will be based on misconceptions about telephone prospecting.

Section 3

4 STEPS TO CONSISTENT SALES THROUGH P2P PROSPECTING

INTRODUCING THE FOUR-STEP METHOD

A S long as the vast majority of today's companies continue to pour their money into online advertising and marketing without investing in a structured prospecting process to complement these digital campaigns, there will be an immense and highly lucrative opportunity for agile, forward-thinking organisations to capture significant market share. P2P prospecting gives those who are prepared to seize the opportunity the power to educate their market, to get below the tip of their iceberg, and to position themselves as the leaders in their field.

The objective of P2P prospecting is to get to your prospects before your competitors and to start a dialogue with them—ideally, just before they start looking for solutions online. To do this, you need two things: the first is a clear picture of your market (you should have this if you followed the process I outlined in the last section); the second is a clear prospecting plan—a structure that dictates how and whom you will call day by day.

Over the past decade, I've developed the four-step method described in this section. I've used it myself, taught it to countless professional prospectors, and it's proved remarkably successful in a wide range of industries. Anyone can use it, and anyone can find success with it. Follow this system to the letter and you too will enjoy a brimming pipeline and sales success unlike anything you've experienced before. None of these steps can be omitted. Miss just one of them and your efforts will fall flat. The four steps are:

1. Define Your Prospecting Value Proposition

2. Refine Your Pitch

3. Streamline Your Process

4. Align Your Follow-Up.

Some of these steps might look familiar. Perhaps you already have a serviceable value proposition. It's also quite likely that your sales team has a working pitch that they're using with some degree of success. That's great. You'll be refining these in the following chapters so they can be used for prospecting. You won't be discarding what you've already got, but that doesn't mean you can skip these steps. Prospecting calls are not sales calls, so your sales pitch won't come into play until later in the process. P2P prospecting calls do occasionally turn into sales calls, but only when the need is apparent and immediate. They aren't forceful or pushy, and they'll be more welcome for this reason. The purpose is not to make immediate sales but, rather, to uncover new sales opportunities. Your sales team are not selling your product or service on these calls, they are selling a meeting; they are selling the next step in your sales process. You'll be using parts of your value proposition and parts of your sales pitch to guide your prospects towards this meeting, but you'll be doing so in an entirely new context.

The four steps we'll be covering in this section will help you engage with prospects in new ways and uncover their needs, but they will also help you qualify potential prospects, making sure they are good prospects for your company. Neglect qualifying and you'll end up wasting your time (and the prospect's as well).

These four steps will not (and should not) replace your existing sales efforts. Rather, they bolt on to the front end of your existing sales process, boosting sales activity and generating new opportunities for your sales team to convert.

There is actually a 'secret' ingredient, without which the whole system will fall down: consistency. No sales system can succeed without day in day out consistency and commitment, and mine is no different. There will be times when it will be tempting to stop. Perhaps your sales people will become frustrated when they don't start making sales immediately, or perhaps your first attempt at defining your market will leave you with a list of unsuitable prospects. Even in the face of incrementally slow progress or setbacks, remain consistent. This is what companies with successful prospecting programmes have learned. They keep going, refining their process and acting on feedback, and this means they improve (either gradually or in leaps and bounds). They coach their sales teams, teaching them how to sell in new ways, making them better-rounded salespeople in the process. They keep going, consistently, and it's this consistency that leads them to great results.

At my company, Forrest Marketing Group, we use this process for ourselves every day, and it works. Over 50% of our new clients come from leads that we have generated through cold calling, and every call we make uses this four-step process. It works for our clients too. We've worked with hundreds of companies over the last decade, and we owe our success to the four-step method and to our consistency.

Sales prospecting will work for you too, and all you have to do is follow these four steps. Let's get started.

Step 1

DEFINE YOUR PROSPECTING VALUE PROPOSITION

B EFORE you make that first call, you need to have a plan. You need to know *exactly* what you're going to say to your prospects when you get them on the line. When you ask yourself what message you want to convey on these calls? The answer: your Prospecting Value Proposition.

A lot has been written about creating a clear Value Proposition for your customers and prospects. Your Value Proposition is the central message that you communicate to your potential customers; having a good one is absolutely vital to sales success, and it will be equally vital if your P2P prospecting is to be successful.

A good Value Proposition boils down to a simple articulation of what a company does, and I am often amazed at people's inability to articulate what they do in simple terms. We've become so dependent on jargon that we struggle to address our customers in language they can instantly understand and connect with. We've all met people at events who, when you ask them what they do, say something cryptic like, "We unlock the human capital of your workforce through capability-based diagnosis." When you're crafting your Prospecting Value Proposition, you'll want to avoid jargon like this. Jargon shrouds what you do or sell in mystery, and you're not Agatha Christie. You're not trying to build suspense. You're trying to be clear and precise.

A good Prospecting Value Proposition is not marketing-speak. It is not a five-minute speech. It is something that can be communicated quickly and clearly. When you are prospecting, the one thing you want to avoid at all costs is a monologue. The best way to avoid long, drawn out speeches is to ask your prospect questions. Your Prospecting Value Proposition introduces your company and your services, but it doesn't stop there. It also includes questions that are designed to open up conversations and uncover needs.

Sometimes, when I am working with a new client and I ask them about what they do, I notice that they forget that they are involved in a conversation. They begin reciting from the company's marketing collateral, and suddenly I feel like I'm being pitched to. I'm no longer in a dialogue—it's a monologue. You might be able to get away with that face to face, but definitely not on the phone. On the phone, you have a very narrow window of opportunity. You have to start the conversation quickly, and you need to cut to the chase immediately.

P2P prospecting uses a conversation to deliver a compelling message that is relevant to, and resonates with, the individuals in your target market. It's about the right message, right person, right time. That's all there is to it. Remember this and your sales prospecting will go well. If you don't, it won't. It really is that simple. Here's a great example of how getting the message wrong can stop a prospecting campaign in its tracks.

A few years ago, we ran a prospecting campaign for a major superannuation provider in Australia. They wanted us to approach owners of SMEs with a maximum of 80 staff. They asked us to present their superannuation product as a way for these companies to become employers of choice in their industry. Now, that sounds well and good (inspirational even), but as it turns out, SME business owners don't really care about being an employer of choice in their industry—not at all. It doesn't even make a blip on their radar. Their challenges and concerns lie elsewhere.

We discovered this within a few hours of starting to make the prospecting calls. Our agents work very hard, and they don't mind working on tough campaigns that might mean working for hours to generate a single, qualified sales lead. They don't throw in the towel until they're well and truly licked, but they came back to us almost immediately, telling us in no uncertain terms that the campaign wasn't working. The client's message just wasn't resonating with the prospects—not remotely.

The problem started and ended with the Prospecting Value Proposition that our client wanted us to deliver. We went back to the client and workshopped their messaging, changing the focus. The results spoke for themselves. The next day, within two hours, we were booking them appointments with the same SME business owners who had turned us down the day before. Different message, different result. This is the power of a good Prospecting Value Proposition.

DEVELOPING YOUR PROSPECTING VALUE PROPOSITION

Your Prospecting Value Proposition is all about your potential customer. It's only obliquely about you. It is first and foremost about their problems—what you can do for them only comes after you have pinpointed their problem. Your Prospecting Value Proposition isn't the same as a Mission or a Vision Statement. It's a succinct description of the benefits your customers enjoy—in short, how you make your customers' lives better or easier. When you are talking to a new prospect on the phone, you don't have time to give a detailed explain of what your company is or does, what you stand for, or what awards you've won.

When crafting your Prospecting Value Proposition, you definitely want to avoid jargon. The terms specific to your industry—be they acronyms, or other industry-specific phrases that describe what you do—should be excluded entirely from your Value Proposition. It's quite likely that the decision maker you're speaking with will be unfamiliar with these terms. As soon as you go over their head, you've lost them. If, for example, you are an IT company and selling to the financial controller or CFO, they will not understand IT jargon, so don't use it. Instead, use simple and direct language, something that a layperson can understand.

You'll deliver your Value Proposition in a short opener that will include a number of pointed questions. These questions will help you hone in on specific needs or issues that you can help them address. To start crafting your Prospecting Value Proposition, ask yourself:

> *What is the pain that my prospects are experiencing that my product or service addresses?*

When you go to the hardware store to buy a drill bit, you're not buying the drill bit, you're buying the hole that it gives you when you use it. So it is with what you're selling. On your prospecting calls, your Prospecting Value Proposition is not about the features of your product or service; it's about the benefits your customers get when they use it. For almost every product or service, this benefit is a solved problem or solved problems. I like to think of it as the pain you take away from your customers.

And remember, it's likely that your prospects are going to have some sort of solution in place for the problem that your products or services solve. Perhaps they're using a competitor's product; perhaps they're making do with a home-baked solution that's been working passably well for some time. Whatever it is, chances are they've got something in place. Your Prospecting Value Proposition needs to take this into account.

Let's have a look at some examples of Prospecting Value Propositions:

Company: ERP Software Provider

Target Market: Companies with 200+ staff. Manufacturing, Wholesale, Mining, Construction, Utilities, Transport and Logistics industries. Target decision maker is the Head of Finance (CFO) and possibly the Head of IT (CIO).

Target Market's Issues: Companies who are using multiple, disparate systems to manage their business find that these systems don't talk to each other easily: their accounting software, CRM, warehouse and inventory or stock control software, supply chain management software, and HR software are all different. To bring the data from these systems together usually requires the use of multiple, complex and interlinked Excel files from each of the organisation's departments. The links between these files frequently break, so that data updated in one file does not update into other files, which leads to highly unreliable data. Maintaining and updating these files is also a very labour-intensive process, requiring many, many man-hours to complete each month. In addition the company cannot get an accurate picture of their position because the time taken to compile all of the figures makes data historical rather that current.

Value Proposition: "We help companies that are using multiple disparate software systems to bring all of their data together into a single company-wide system. We get rid of the multiple Excel files that many rely on to give them the information they need to manage their business, and we save the companies hundreds of man hours because they no longer have to collate, maintain and verify data to ensure it is correct. Our clients get accurate, up-to-date information covering all areas of their organisation, at all times."

Company: Debtor Finance Provider

Target Market: Companies with 20-200 staff. Manufacturing, Wholesale, Construction, Transport and Logistics, Information Media and Telecommunications, Rental, Hire and Real Estate, Administration and Support, Professional, Scientific and Technical Services industries. Decision maker is the Head of Finance in larger organisations or the Business Owner in smaller companies.

Target Market's Issues: Pressure on their cash flow from the increasing time taken by clients to pay their invoices. This can make it hard to pay their staff and suppliers on time, which means they risk losing their top talent and key staff. Ultimately this can lead to the failure of the business.

Value Proposition: "We help companies with clients who are taking longer and longer to pay them. We take away the stress of having to chase clients for payment by paying invoices as soon as they are issued. That means they don't have to worry about losing their key staff because they can't pay their wages, or about losing good suppliers because they can't pay their bills. We allow our clients to focus on building really good businesses."

Company: Office Coffee Machine Provider

Target Market: Companies with 10-80 staff. All industries except Agriculture, Retail, Accommodation and Food, Education, Healthcare, Arts and Recreation. Decision maker is the Business Owner.

Target Market's Issues: Staff productivity due to time lost by staff continually leaving the office to get their coffee throughout the day. Staff may buy two or three coffees each per day, leaving the office for 10-15 minutes each time they do so. Going for coffee becomes a social activity, so staff often go out in groups, which stretches these breaks even further. For a company with 20 staff, this is equivalent to over 140 hours of lost time every month.

Value Proposition: "We help companies increase staff productivity and motivation by installing our coffee machines in their kitchens, giving them access to great coffee at work. This stops your team from constantly having to spend time going out to a coffee van or nearby coffee shop throughout the day and maximises their productive time at work."

As you can see, these Prospecting Value Propositions are not about product or service features. Instead, they focus on the key problems that the seller can solve for the purchaser. These problems are not always immediately obvious, so it helps to spend some time thinking about what issues you can help your customers solve.

You can see the results of this problem-centric thinking in the case study for the coffee machine provider. The obvious Value Proposition for this company is quite simple: they provide high-quality coffee for staff members. But that message will not resonate with the decision makers in their target market. Just like the superannuation company, employers don't really care about whether their staff have good-tasting coffee or not. It doesn't really register for them as a priority, so the obvious Value Proposition has little prospecting value. This is where some creative thinking makes the difference. You wouldn't usually think of a coffee machine as a productivity tool, but that is what it is or can be in the eyes of the customers that you sell to. As soon as you connect the product to a more pressing issue (in this case, staff productivity), you've got their attention, and perhaps their business as well. The more obvious Value Proposition (we give your staff great coffee) can remain unstated, or at the most mentioned as an added benefit.

Don't be put off by trying to make your Value Proposition too short. You'll see from the above examples, that none of them are less than a few sentences long. They're not sound bites, but they're not paragraphs either. Strike a balance that will allow you to clearly explain the value of what you're selling in layman's terms without droning on and on. Getting it right will probably mean a few sentences. If you need three or four sentences, try to keep each of them relatively short.

In his book, *NewSell*, Michael Hewitt-Gleeson says that to sell effectively you need to change a prospect's Current View of the Situation (CVS) to a Better View of the Situation (BVS). All you need to do is make your product or service the catalyst for that movement from CVS to BVS.

I like to do this in three steps:

1. Identify their pain (their CVS)
2. List the questions you can ask that will uncover this pain
3. Refine your Prospecting Value Proposition so that it highlights how your products/services address this pain (show them a BVS).

This should take no more than 30 minutes to complete. Start by dividing a piece of paper into three columns. Label these columns "CVS", "?", and "BVS". In the left column, list as many of your prospect's pain points as you can. Don't filter them at this stage; just get them all down on paper. There will be different ones for different types of prospects. A prospect who has been a client in the past may have different pain points from a prospect you haven't worked with before. A prospect who has their own in-house solution in place will have pain points very different from a prospect that is using your competitor's products or services. List them all. You can put a "C" (using a competitor), or a "P" (a prospect) or a "D" (a dormant account) beside questions that only apply to that one group if that makes it easier.

Keep circling back to the question, "What is the problem (that is, the pain) my prospects experience each day?" The trick is to look at this from the prospect's perspective, not from yours. This can be difficult if you haven't yet tried to walk a mile in your prospect's shoes, noticing where they rub and pinch. Thinking about your Prospecting Value Proposition at this stage and in this way will pay dividends later on.

Once you've identified all of your prospects' pain points, you can start trying to fit your product or service to the issue. How can you take away their pain, make their life better, make their business more profitable? Match the benefits of your product or service with each of the pain points you have written down. Write these down in the right column across from their corresponding pain point. If the same benefit appears across from multiple pain points, you're on the right track.

Here's an example of how this might look for a B2B company that provides outsourced payroll solutions. The target decision maker is the Head of Finance or the business owner, depending on company size.

You'll see that there is some repetition in the questions that can be asked and the BVS that these can lead the conversation towards. This kind of overlapping is a good sign. The more pain points your questions can uncover, the better. In this instance, just a couple of questions are able to uncover a wide range of payroll challenges.

CVS	Discovery questions	BVS
The company must have one or more staff member dedicated to processing payroll.	How much time is spent processing payroll each month? As you grow, will you need more staff to process the payroll? Is the time taken to do this stopping your staff from completing other important tasks? How much do you spend on processing payroll per month just now?	The entire payroll function is looked after by us, so your staff can focus on other duties and tasks. There is no need to add more staff to your payroll team as the company grows. We can scale up and down with you. We can handle all of your payroll and superannuation payments from as little as $xxx per employee per pay cycle, saving you money throughout the year.
Additional time is required to manage superannuation payments across multiple superannuation funds.	How many different superannuation funds do you have to make payments to each quarter? How much time is spent processing all of these payments? Is the time taken to do this stopping your staff from completing other important tasks?	All of your superannuation payments are handled by us, so your team doesn't have to handle payments to multiple funds. Your staff have time to focus on other duties/ tasks. We can handle all of your payroll and Superannuation payments from as little as $xxx per employee per pay cycle, saving you money throughout the year.

CVS	Discovery questions	BVS
It is difficult to maintain compliance with penalty rates and overtime.	Do you have staff working overtime or staff who can be on penalty rates? How often do these rates not get applied correctly? How much time does your staff spend ensuring that the business remains current with all of the payroll and Superannuation legislation? How much time is spent trying to manage this system?	Our systems make sure that all staff get paid the correct rates, and that overtime and penalty rates get correctly applied every time. No more sleepless nights for you or your team worrying about under or overpaying staff. Your staff can stop attending training and refresher courses to maintain current with payroll, superannuation and award rate legislation. They will have more time to focus on other tasks and duties.
Staff members are paid incorrectly.	How often do you have staff who are either underpaid or overpaid thanks to payroll calculation mistakes? How much time does it take to fix this up each time? How do your staff feel when they aren't paid their wages correctly?	No more sleepless nights for you or your team worrying about under or overpaying staff. No more costly re-running of the payroll to fix up mistakes. Your staff members are going to be correctly paid the first time every time. They will spend less time double-checking their pay, and they will be much happier at work.

Once you have a good list like the one here, review what you have done. Are there any pain points that you don't have a solution (a BVS) for? This is where creative thinking (think of the coffee example above) will make all the difference. The more serious the issue, the more important it is that you find a way that your product or service addresses it. Are there any benefits you have listed that don't address any of the pain points? If so, are these really benefits you want to highlight (think about the superannuation company above)? If even creative thinking can't help you connect a benefit to a pain point, delete the benefit from your list or set it aside for brainstorming another day.

Now let's turn our attention to the middle column, where you need to list the questions that bridge the gap between each problem and its solution. If you can think of multiple questions that do this for some of the problems, that's great. Sometimes, getting the answer you're looking for means asking two or three similar or related questions.

Finally, review the questions on your list. Remember that these questions will be the backbone of your prospecting conversations, so it's important that they're clear and concise. It's also important that you don't phrase them in such a way that the prospect will feel like they're being led by the nose to give a particular answer (even if that is what you are doing). They should feel genuine. They should also be open questions where possible (questions that don't require a yes or no answer). If your first draft is full of closed questions, go through the list and revise them so they cannot be answered with a simple yes or no. A good way to do this is to make sure that each of them starts with Who, What, Where, When, Why, How (much/often). Try not to have too many questions that start with Why, though. Why questions are open-ended, but they can be easily misinterpreted as confrontational. Deliver why questions indelicately and you'll soon be holding a dead line. Even if delivered in the right way, they're risky. Rapport is so important at this stage that you'll want to avoid *anything* that risks a communication breakdown.

Once you have completed this step you should be able to identify three things:

1. Your prospects' pain
2. How your product or service can address this pain
3. Questions that will help you get the prospect talking about their pain and lead you into a conversation about your solution.

This (a short opening statement followed by a number of questions designed to uncover the prospect's issues) is your Prospecting Value Proposition, and it is the foundation upon which you'll be building your prospecting calls and the sales approach that will follow. The next step is to develop an approach that will allow you to engage the prospect in a structured conversation—one that will allow you to ask the questions you have just created. Crucially, though, we need to do this in a way that avoids turning the call into an interrogation. I'll cover this in the next chapter.

Chapter summary

- Since you'll be starting each call with a short introduction, you'll need to develop a clear and engaging Prospecting Value Proposition.

- Avoid using jargon or other mystifying language. Opt instead for clear and direct language that conveys precisely what you do or sell.

- Your Prospecting Value Proposition should focus on your potential customers' issues and how your organisation will address and solve these issues for them.

- The main question your Prospecting Value Proposition should answer is, "How do you make your customers' lives better or easier?"

- Start by asking yourself the following question: What is the pain that my prospects are experiencing that my product or service addresses?

- Your Prospecting Value Proposition should make it clear to the prospect how your product or service will take them from a Current View of the Situation (CVS) to a Better View of the Situation (BVS).

- The questions you'll want to ask as part of your Prospecting Value Proposition should form a bridge between the CVS and the BVS.

- Try to see what you are selling from the prospect's perspective. Try to walk a mile in their shoes and imagine where their shoes rub or pinch.

- Use open-ended questions (questions that can't be answered with a yes or no). This will give the prospect the opportunity to provide detailed answers. This will help you ask follow-up questions in ways that feel perfectly natural.

- Avoid why questions. They can feel confrontational, and this stage is all about building a rapport with the prospect.

REFINE YOUR PITCH

NOW, with your market clearly defined and your Prospecting Value Proposition in hand, it's time to turn to developing a dynamite pitch. This means working on (or perhaps developing for the first time) your prospecting script. The word "script" tends to set salespeople's teeth on edge. They imagine themselves being turned into robots, pitching by rote. This is where assumptions about what prospecting is or should be lead people astray. They imagine that the script will need to cover everything they might say during a prospecting call, but this just isn't the case. When I use the word "script" I don't mean something that is read line by line on every call. I mean a platform that your sales team can use to build a meaningful conversation with each prospect they talk to, regardless of what that prospect's pain or needs are. These conversations should be anything but "scripted".

The truth is that we all have scripts. Actors have scripts, and if they're good actors, we believe them when they are in character. They don't sound like they are reading words off a page, but that's essentially what they're doing (and, like good salespeople, they're ad-libbing more than you might realise). Salespeople have scripts too. Good salespeople have their scripts in their heads, and they're constantly being revised and honed to a fine point. They've developed them over years and years of selling. The best salespeople adapt their script to each situation, each conversation, each prospect. The trick is to develop a script that is malleable, able to be adapted according to your prospects' specific situations and needs.

There are many ways that you can do this. The approach that we use, and that I recommend, will allow you to engage with your prospects easily. There are two key ingredients to this approach. The first is the use of good questions that get the prospect talking—and talking as early in the conversation as possible. The second ingredient is a mindset: I want you to treat the prospecting call as a discovery call, not a sales call.

Let's start by looking at the first ingredient.

The approach that many people take on the phone involves taking a deep breath and talking *at* the prospect (as opposed to *with* them). Poor salespeople do this because they want to tell the prospect everything about their product or service, hoping that the prospect will hear something in the pitch that catches their attention. They list the product's features at length, counting the call as a success if they can get to the end of their spiel without the prospect interrupting them. At the end of their pitch, if the prospect doesn't ask for information, they launch into yet another monologue. This isn't a conversation, and it smacks of desperation. People don't like this approach. They know they are being pitched to and their defences go up. They refuse to engage and they often stop listening entirely. Even if they have a need, this approach won't uncover it.

This type of approach is about as effective as playing the same recorded message to every prospect. It doesn't work, not, at least, with enough people to make the effort worthwhile. This is the kind of prospecting that *will* damage your brand, and it will almost certainly put your sales team off prospecting. I can't urge you strongly enough against this approach. Start talking at the submerged part of your iceberg rather than with them and you'll be wasting your opportunity.

Instead of talking at prospects, you want to engage them in a conversation, and you do this by asking them questions about their current situation. Get them talking to you, not the other way around. Build your pitch around fact-finding more than around informing, and this is where the second ingredient of good prospecting calls comes into play. Think about these calls as discovery calls rather than sales calls and the prospect will feel the difference (and react differently). The objective of a discovery call should be to find out the following about the prospect:

- Are they a valid prospect or not?
- What is the prospect's current situation?
- Where are they in the buying cycle?

Let's look at each of these questions in turn.

Are they a valid prospect?

The first thing you want to know is whether a company is actually a worthwhile prospect for you. Are they actually part of your iceberg, or are you wasting your time (and theirs)? Can they afford your services? Can they benefit from them? You'll want to uncover the answers to these questions quickly but discreetly.

A prospect who is not interested today is not the same as a prospect who is not in your market. Don't eliminate someone from your iceberg just because they are not interested today. Perhaps they are happily using a competitor's product right now, but customers, we know, are fickle. These prospects are absolutely still part of your iceberg. They're just not ready to buy yet, but they might buy at some point down the track. You only eliminate a prospect if they really don't have a need for what you sell, or if they don't meet your minimum client profile and are unlikely to grow to that profile. Qualifying your prospects in this way is an extremely important part of the process, so we'll talk more about it at the end of this chapter.

What is the prospect's current situation?

During the call, you should be trying to find out what each individual prospect is doing today (their CVS). Prospects aren't always forthcoming about their needs, so we gather information about their current situation. This usually points us in the direction of a need or issue. The questions that you developed in the last chapter will become the foundation for this. You want to use these questions to gather as much information about the prospect as you can. What solution are they currently using, and for how long have they been using it? How many (if any) of the pain points that you identified in the last chapter are they experiencing? What are the challenges they are facing with their current solution? Finally, how big a client will the company likely be for you if you can win their business? This is a key piece of information that will allow you to tailor your approach to not just their need but also the size of this need. It will also keep you from wasting too much time on barely-qualified prospects. If the account is not going to be a relatively big one, an online demo or phone appointment might be all that is appropriate. If the account has much larger potential, face-to-face meetings will become appropriate.

Where are they in the buying cycle?

Not everyone who is part of your iceberg is going to want to buy from you now. In fact, we find that normally, depending on the product or service, only between 5% and 20% of qualified prospects have a current need. The remaining 80% to 95% of your qualified prospects will not be ready to buy today. That doesn't make them bad prospects—quite the contrary, these are your future clients.

Your salespeople will need to be briefed on these numbers, especially if they are used to selling exclusively to warm or hot prospects. Sharing these numbers will help when you're discussing expectations with your team. Finding out where your prospects are in the buying cycle will determine when and how you will follow up with them. You can start sending great marketing material that is completely relevant to each prospect at the appropriate times, and you can combine this with follow-up phone calls so that, when the time is right, your sales team is right there to convert that prospect into a client.

By using these three questions as the focus of your prospecting you'll be building the foundations for a multi-million dollar sales pipeline. You will know whether or not they are suitable prospects, you'll know who they actually are, what issues they are dealing with, and you'll know when they are likely to buy. By knowing the answers to these three questions, you can segment prospects into sub-groups: who is interested in what, how big an account they will be, and when are they likely to buy. You can re-engage with them at the appropriate time with an approach tailored to their likely sale value and product or service of interest. You'll be building trust, and when they are ready to purchase, you'll be in pole position.

STRUCTURING YOUR SCRIPT

Let's get back to the script—or, if you prefer, the discovery platform. How should your prospecting call be structured? It should be simple, and it should be in three stages:

1. Introduction

2. Questions to build a conversation

3. Wrap-up.

Let's look more closely at each of these.

Introduction

On a prospecting call, you want your prospect to be doing most of the talking, so you want to use only two sentences, at most three, to introduce yourself. When I've coached people through this process, they've often started with a series of three-line sentences or even a paragraph that covers an entire page. This misses the point entirely. Your sentences should be short, direct and clear (as a good general guideline, they shouldn't be any longer than a tweet). After that, the prospect should be the one talking, with your questions guiding the dialogue. Once you're through the introduction, you can use some of the pain-uncovering questions you prepared in the last chapter.

To help you along, here are a few examples that we've used for clients.

Hello [NAME], it's Richard from XYZ company.

We're a debtor finance company. We help companies that are struggling to get their customers to pay them on time. What we do is give them access to funds as soon as the invoice is raised, rather than having to wait 30 or 60 days for payment.

> *Hello [NAME] it's Richard from XYZ company.*
>
> *We provide a complete supply chain risk management solution. We help our clients ensure that their suppliers and contractors are fully compliant with current legislation and that they remain compliant throughout their relationship with you.*

> *Hello [NAME], it's Richard from XYZ company.*
>
> *We are part of a leading insurance broking network, and we help businesses find insurance solutions that manage their business risks better. We work with a range of insurance companies, making sure you're getting the best possible coverage and potentially reducing your insurance policy costs.*

Got the idea? Keep your introduction short and sweet, using punchy sentences that make it clear from the outset who you are and how you help your customers. After your introduction, you'll want to start asking questions immediately, but you need to approach this carefully. Let's look at how to do this.

Questions to build a conversation

Clearly, you can't just dive straight into asking questions. Well, you *can*, but you *shouldn't*. Having a flow to the conversation is important, and jumping right into questions will make the prospect feel like they're being dragged into a whirlpool.

This is one of the reasons sales people who talk *at* the prospect fail so frequently. They convey an assumption that the prospect has a pronounced and already obvious need for their service. Maybe they don't.

In fact, it's quite possible that, at the start of the call, they don't think they have a problem at all. So the talking-at-the-prospect approach is going to put you offside before you even begin.

How we avoid this is simple. It's a very quick line that I learnt from Ari Galper, a great sales trainer. It works well because it is disarming. Immediately after your introduction, say this:

> *"Now, I don't know enough about your situation to know if something like this would make sense for you, so would it be okay if I asked you a couple of quick questions?"*

Now, pause and wait for the prospect to respond with a yes. They will almost always give you the go-ahead, unless they are busy and would prefer that you call back at a more convenient time. Once you get that yes, you have been given their permission to start a conversation. Let me show you how this works using one of my clients as an example:

> *Hello [NAME], it's Richard from XYZ company.*
>
> *We help businesses maximise returns on their excess industrial assets by selling these for them on our online auction website. We auction a diverse range of assets, from office furniture and cars to major mining and civil equipment and infrastructure.*
>
> *Right now, we're looking for people who are open to having a chat about how they can better manage their stock levels and free up cash flow by disposing of excess assets.*
>
> *Now, I don't know enough about your situation to know if something like this would make sense for you, so would it be okay if I asked you a couple of quick questions?*

You'll notice the extra sentence between the introduction and the question prompter here. This sentence can also be used to qualify prospects at the beginning of the call, so that your sales team doesn't waste its time talking to prospects at length, only to find out at the end of the conversation that the prospect isn't qualified (I'll talk more about this in the next section).

Next, you can turn back to the questions that you developed in the last chapter. As you're writing your pitch, you'll want to include these questions, and you will need to think about the order in which you ask them. As a rule, you want to start with broad, easy to answer questions and then move on to more focused questions as the conversation develops. Start with questions that are most likely to uncover *any* issues a prospect might have. The order of the questions should flow naturally. It should, if possible, feel as though the prospect's answers to the first question lead you to ask the second one, and so on. Use linking words and phrases like "And..." and "Okay, so..." to make the questions feel more like a conversation and less like an interrogation.

Can you have too many questions? Absolutely, but most people start with too few, not too many. The questions need to identify the pain in the current situation (or the opportunity), so you need to ask more (rather than less) of them. Remember that your sales team will not ask all of the questions all of the time. The questions should be prompts for them. Once they start uncovering issues, they can develop the conversation further, focusing on a specific issue and asking the questions that reveal as much detail as possible about that problem and how it's affecting the prospect's business. If you find that your sales team find themselves jumping between questions rather than following them in order, this is absolutely fine—indeed, this is how they *should* be used. It is an indication that your sales team are developing the *right* conversation with each prospect.

Using questions to build the conversation is how your sales team can demonstrate that they understand each prospect's unique situation. They'll be guiding the prospect towards the solution they're selling, and, what is more, they'll be building a relationship with them. If you select your questions carefully (being sure to discard ones that aren't working), you'll find yourself having more productive and relationship-building conversations with your prospects. Choose them carelessly and you'll come off as just another telemarketer, and, after all the work you have put in so far, that is the *last* thing you want.

Below, you'll find some of the questions that we used for one of our clients (an Australian company with a team of business coaches). We grouped the questions into three main issues that business owners in the industry typically grapple with: time (working too many hours), team (not being able to build a strong team around themselves) and money (not making enough of it). We approach prospects on the assumption that they may have at least one, but possibly all three, of these issues. We don't want to miss an opportunity by focussing our questions on just, say, money issues. You may find that your prospects also have pain points in a number of other areas. You'll need a series of questions for each area, so this example will help you to see how you should structure these questions for your sales team.

In the following example, which we have used to generate hundreds of appointments, you will notice that our opening question is really broad. A broad first question is the best way to get the prospect to open up early in the conversation. If their answer doesn't reveal anything usable, we then move to more specific questions, asking whether time, team or money is their main issue, but still leaving the door open to the possibility that it is something else entirely. On the next three pages you'll see short lists of more detailed questions that dig deep into each of the three main issues. We use these when we strike pay dirt (that is, when the prospect reveals an issue in one of the particular problem areas).

You'll see I include a prompt to "act dumb and dig deep" throughout the script. This is a reminder to prospectors that they need to keep asking questions until they have really identified the pain and the level of frustration that the prospect is experiencing, rather than just jumping to the close as soon as it appears there is an issue in one area. Get the prospect to recognise their pain by digging deep and you'll get much better sales leads.

AREAS OF FRUSTRATION – SAMPLE PITCH

[INTRO]

Now I don't know enough about your situation to know if something like that might make sense for you, so would it be ok if I ask you a couple of questions?

1. *So, if you look at your company's situation right now, what would you say is the single biggest challenge/frustration that you face?* **Go to appropriate area of frustration**

2. *Well, many of the clients we work with have frustrations with working long hours, not having enough money each month, or having team members that they have to constantly supervise or fix their problems. Is it one of those three things for you, or is it something else?* **Go to appropriate area of frustration**

3. *So, in your opinion, what would you say is causing that?*

4. *Okay, and what are the consequences to your business—and to you personally—if the problem isn't solved and the current situation drags on?*

If they say everything is fine:

1. *What's one thing that you'd really like to achieve or improve in your business in the next 90 days?*

2. *What are you doing to achieve that just now?*

3. *How likely is it that you will achieve this?*

AREAS OF FRUSTRATION – ACT DUMB AND DIG DEEP

Area 1: Time

1. *So how many hours do you work each week?*
   If less than 45 hours per week, go to "Money" or "Team"

2. *And how many evenings and weekends do you work? How do you feel about that?*

3. *Do you have a family, [name]? How do they feel about the kind of hours you're working?*

4. *Is this taking away time that you should really be spending with your wife/family?*

5. *So what's stopping you from working fewer hours?*

6. *And what happens when you take a holiday?*

7. *So what would it mean to you if you could get more time back for yourself/take a holiday when you wanted?*

*So, if we could show you some strategies around getting more time back for yourself **AND** making sure that the business continues to grow, that would be worth you looking at, wouldn't it?*

Well, people who've been working with [COMPANY NAME] have typically been able to reduce their hours from 70 to 80 per week to between 30 and 40 per week, and many of them have started taking regular holidays, often within as little as six months.

AREAS OF FRUSTRATION – ACT DUMB AND DIG DEEP

Area 2: Money

1. Are you happy with the amount of money you are taking from the business for yourself? How much more would you like to be taking home?

2. What kind of stress is your current income level creating at home?

3. Are your employees making more money than you are? How do you feel about that?

4. And what are you doing at the moment to grow your business?

5. On a scale of 1 to 10, how hard is your business running just now? Is it realising its full potential, or is it running at 50%? 60%?

6. How much growth do you think your business could handle?

7. If you had more money (and the time to enjoy it), what would you do?

8. Would that be a top priority (for a coach) to work on?

So, if we could show you some strategies that would allow you to take more money from the business for yourself while also increasing your turnover and profits, that would be worth taking a look at, wouldn't it? Now, you said you'd like to see a _____% growth in your profits. Well, businesses we're working with and who have followed our strategies have typically achieved a growth in profits of **60–80%** within their first year. Some have even seen 140–150% growth.

AREAS OF FRUSTRATION – ACT DUMB AND DIG DEEP

Area 3: Team

1. *How happy are you with your team? How does their commitment (to the business) compare with yours?*

2. *What would you most like to change about your team?*

3. *If you had to start from scratch, how many of your existing staff members would you hire again?*

4. *Do you have a high staff turnover? How often do you lose people and have to replace them? What's causing this?*

5. *How well would you say your team runs the business when you take a 2-3 week holiday?*

6. *When was the last time you took a 2-3 week holiday? What's stopping you from doing this?*

7. *Do have the right people in place in the key positions in the company?*

8. *What would it mean to you to have a team you could rely on?*

9. *If you had the right team/someone you could delegate some of your responsibilities to, what would you do with that extra time?*

10. *What would it mean to you to be able to take a long holiday and spend more time with your family?*

So, if we could show you some strategies around building a great team that you could really rely on, that would be worth looking at, wouldn't it? Well, businesses we're working with have been able to cut down staff turnover and build really strong teams that are able to run the business while the owner is on holiday.

As you can see, the script flows smoothly and naturally from beginning to end. However, this doesn't mean that members of my team read it end to end when they are prospecting. It's simply not meant to be used this way. Invariably, one of these questions starts a more detailed conversation. At key moments in the conversation (particularly when the conversation slows down), a new question is asked, and this keeps things rolling along smoothly. We might use the next question on the list, or we might use the last one—it depends on the conversation. This is P2P prospecting. It's a conversational selling technique that has proven to be far more effective than pitching by rote can ever be. It's an approach that is relevant and adaptable, and this is what makes it such a powerful selling tool.

Once we have found out which area is causing pain, we focus on that pain. With a list of questions like those I've provided above, our prospectors can feel comfortable on any call and in any situation with any kind of prospect. Whatever the prospect's issue, we have a question close at hand that can draw that issue out of them, and then, once they've caught the scent, they have further questions that will help draw more crucial information out of the prospect. If one of these questions reveals yet more pressing issues elsewhere, we can change gears in an instant, moving to the area that is rubbing or pinching the most. It's then merely a matter of showing the prospect that their issue can be and should be addressed (and, most importantly, that our client can and should be the one to address it).

Remember that when you are writing a script for your team, you are not writing it to be read. You are writing it to be spoken. The biggest mistake people make when writing scripts is that they try to make it read well, and they forget that it is being delivered over the phone as a conversation. When you write a script for your sales team, or when you review one that has been written for them by someone else, read it aloud and time how long it takes to get through it. More than 15 seconds for the introduction is too long. In most cases, 10-12 seconds is the Goldilocks zone.

Wrap-up

This is straightforward, so I won't spend much time on it. This is where you ask the prospect to take the next step with you. If the prospect is interested, the next step you want to guide them towards might be meeting to discuss your offer, it might be attending an event or a webinar, or it might be watching a web demo highlighting your product's features. Remember, though, there are also next steps for qualified prospects who don't have an immediate need or even interest. You might want to call back in a few weeks or in a few months (much longer than six months and they probably won't recall you or the conversation). If this is the case, you'll want to use the wrap up part of the conversation to ask for an email address where you can stay in touch with them (via a newsletter or other e-marketing materials) in between calls.

The simplest way to transition to the wrap-up is to restate their needs. Re-stating their needs shows that you have listened to, and understood, their needs, and it reminds the prospect of exactly why they *should* take the next step with you. This should make asking them to take the next step relatively natural. This doesn't need to be pushy. If you have uncovered the prospect's pain, they should be keen to take the next step too. Here's an example of how you can do this. I'm going to stay with the business coaching example so you can see how the wrap-up brings together what has already been discussed.

*Well [name], based on what you've told me, you're looking to... [RESTATE THEIR NEEDS] and this is **exactly** what we can help you to achieve.*

It might make sense, if you have a bit of time (maybe say 45 minutes to an hour), for you to meet with one of our business coaches, just to have a look at what you're doing now and for him to be able to give you some ideas you can use right away—if you'd be open to that.

*Okay, I'll organise an hour-long introductory meeting with one of our coaches. During that time, he'll be able to get a really clear picture of where you're at and where you want to go and he'll be able to see **exactly** how to help you achieve what you want in your business.*

So now we have covered how you should introduce the call, ask questions that uncover the prospect's pain, and wrap up the conversation. There's still one more particularly important thing we need to slot into the script: qualification.

QUALIFYING PROSPECTS

Remember, one of the top priorities during prospecting is ensuring that you are, in fact, talking to a qualified potential customer. This takes some degree of tact, but you will still need to approach qualifying questions directly. Do this in the right way and you'll be building a database full of qualified prospects that you can nurture until they are ready to buy. Neglect qualifying and you'll be wasting your or your sales team's time.

What "qualified" means to you will depend largely on what you're selling, and it's important you don't fall into the trap of assuming that qualified only means that the prospect can afford your solution. Here are a few qualifying topics you'll probably want to introduce into the conversation:

Organisation size

This will give you some idea about the potential size of the account. Depending on your industry, you may want to know the number of seats or users (if you supply IT solutions), the number of tradespeople working on the tools (if you are a trade supply company), the number of people in a specific, relevant department (Sales, Marketing, IT, etc.) or in the entire company.

Approximate annual turnover

This can be a difficult piece of information to get, and even seasoned salespeople often feel uncomfortable asking prospects direct questions about their annual turnover. You *can't* ask about annual turnover at the beginning of a call—you need to build rapport and trust first. If it's a necessary qualifying question (and it often is), save it for close to the end of the call.

The best approach is to ask prospects which band their turnover falls into. For instance:

- Less than $5 million
- $5 million to $20 million
- $20 million to $50 million
- $50 million to $100 million
- More than $100 million.

These are just arbitrary bands that you can define for your own specific market. In this case, the minimum qualifying turnover would be $5 million. The other bands help determine precisely what kind of customer the prospect will be and what solution will be appropriate for them.

Let's say that your clients need to have a minimum annual turnover of $4 million, you can ask them if their annual turnover exceeds that minimum cut-off. However, remember that people don't want to be seen as "not good enough", so they may inflate their turnover slightly so that they appear to fit the right profile. So, when we ask this question, we usually add a buffer of 20% or so to ensure they *do* fit into the band that we need them to. If the minimum turnover needs to be $4 million, we might ask prospects if their annual turnover exceeds $5 million.

Another way to get an indication of annual turnover is to ask them how many staff they have (much easier to ask than questions about their turnover). A good rule of thumb is that for every $120,000 in annual revenue, the company will probably have one FTE (full-time equivalent) staff member. As the number of staff grows, this rule of thumb becomes less reliable, but for companies with between three and 100 staff, staff numbers will give you a good rough estimate of turnover.

Current situation

What is each prospect doing or using now that your solution would replace? They may have an in-house solution, or they may be using one of your competitor's products, or they may have no solution in place at all. By knowing this, you can get some idea whether or not they will make a good customer (especially if the solution you're offering costs about as much or less than the one your competitor offers).

It's also helpful to know how long they've been using that solution. A company that has only recently bought from, or engaged with, one of your competitors has been through a time-consuming process to choose that supplier—and it's safe to assume that they've spent a considerable amount of money on that purchase. Companies will always need time to use your competitor's product or service before they'll be willing to consider making a change. It's only at this point that talking to them again will be worthwhile. They're not likely to buy from you before they've encountered some issues (small or large) with their new or existing solution. Schedule a call back appropriately. Depending on the product, this might be in three months, or it might be longer, so be sure to nurture them with marketing collateral in the interim.

Are they under contract?

This information is very important when contracts are the norm within your industry. It also applies in any situation where companies have an annually or otherwise regularly renewed policy (for example, business insurance, phones, etc.). Knowing the expiry date of a contract or policy allows you to call the prospect back a few months before their contract expires. This will be a good window in which you can get to know the prospect, build a relationship with them, and pitch your services to them at the ideal moment.

You might think that this would be an obvious piece of information to collect, and it is, but even though we take our clients through a fairly wide-ranging strategy brief, we have still had clients who have not informed us that the prospects that we are calling for them may be under contract. We've wasted everybody's time booking appointments with prospects that are not yet viable prospects. If this is going to be a factor in your prospecting, be sure that, as early in the call as possible, your salespeople ask prospects whether or not they are currently under contact. If they are, these prospects can be fed back into the pipeline. They can be called again when their contract expiry date is visible on the horizon.

Frequency and size of order

Knowing how often a prospect orders from your competitor and the relative (or exact) size of these orders will allow you to define the potential value of the account. Like annual turnover, some prospects might feel uncomfortable answering direct questions about order size and frequency, but they are more likely to give you this information than they are to tell you exactly how much they are spending right now, so it is well worth asking these types of questions. There are often indirect ways to find out what you need to know (for example, if you are in logistics, the number and destination of pallets or containers shipped each week will allow you to estimate this information).

Now it can be frustrating to spend time talking to a prospect, only to discover when you get round to qualifying them at the end of the call that, for whatever reason, they are not a suitable prospect for you. Here is a simple way to get around this. In the last section, I included a sentence starting with "Right now we are looking for people who…" in the one of the introduction scripts. Rather than waiting for the end of the call to qualify the prospect, you can use a sentence like this to determine whether or not the call should continue. Making sure you're dealing with qualified prospects early in the conversation can often save your sales team time a tremendous amount of time.

Let's say you provide IT software to architectural firms, and you know that only companies with at least 10 architects are suitable candidates for your software. You could qualify companies at the beginning of the call by using the following at the end of your introduction:

> *Right now we're looking for companies that have 10 or more architects who are storing files in multiple locations and are finding it hard to manage version control across their projects.*

If unqualified prospects are paying attention, they'll almost always tell you right away that they're not qualified. At this point, politely end the call and move on to the next (hopefully qualified) prospect. You can use this same approach with your existing prospects (those who have been receiving marketing messages for some time) and dormant accounts. There very well might be untapped potential right under your nose—or you might be barking up the wrong tree.

Here's an example of what I mean. We were calling the dormant accounts of a well-known trade supplier. These were customers who hadn't ordered in the last two years, and none of them had, when they were active accounts, spent more than $20,000 per year with our client. To estimate the size of each potential account, we asked each company how many staff they had working "on the tools". Our client had told us that, on average, a customer would spend $29,000 with them for each tradesperson they had working on the tools. Very early on in the campaign, we called a company that told us they had 32 people working on the tools. That's a million-dollar account right there. Up to that point, our client thought it was an account worth less than $20,000. It had been sitting there, right under their noses, for two years. Nobody from the organisation had contacted them about placing an order. They'd effectively let two million dollars in sales slip through their fingers.

Online marketing would never have discovered this. Qualifying prospects without a conversation at the centre of the sales process amounts to little more than guesswork.

Be aware that information you gather when qualifying prospects is not set in stone. Organisations grow and needs change over time. Timelines move forward or backward; companies expand and contract. There's no point at which qualifying should stop. It's got to be an ongoing process to be really effective. It's good to have confidence in your pipeline, but it's always helpful to make sure nothing has dramatically changed in the prospect's organisation in between calls. Any change in the prospect's situation should be checked during your ongoing nurturing calls and noted in the prospect's record in your CRM.

An effective script, with a structured approach to the introduction (including qualifying), the conversation-producing questions, and the wrap-up, is vital to the success of your prospecting. Leave any of these components out and you'll be making it more difficult to gain traction out there. Prospecting isn't easy work, so don't make it harder for yourself or your sales team. Hone your introduction down to a fine point; start a dialogue through pointed questions that uncover problems; don't forget to qualify the prospect; guide the prospect towards the next step. Do all of these things in the right way and you'll soon be enjoying a pipeline brimming with lucrative opportunities.

Your sales team might not be comfortable at first with this process. They're probably not used to prospecting in this way, and they might be resistant to calling prospects and working with a script. They might be convinced they have a better way to prospect, and if they are, they might just go ahead and put their own approach into practice. You'll want to strongly discourage this. Consistency isn't just about applying the same methods over time; it's also about the same methods being applied by *everybody* in your organisation. The best way to overcome this is to involve them in the script-writing process. The more input they have into the precise wording of the script, the more likely you'll get their buy-in.

Check in with your salespeople regularly. They might slowly stop using the script. Over time, it's not uncommon for salespeople to do this, adapting the pitch to their own style of selling. After six months or a year, their script probably won't remotely resemble the one they started with. This too should be strongly discouraged. While the fine details can (and should) be adjusted to suit the person making the call, the main thrust of the pitch should remain the same. Periodically listen in on your salespeople's calls, making sure they're sticking to the script you've developed with them. After all, actors don't change the script each time they get up on stage. They stick with the words that they know convey the playwright's energy, passion and plot. They might flub a word or two here or there, but the thrust of each line remains the same. While the thrust remains the same, the play can be counted upon to pack the house. The same principle applies in sales. Get the script right and, once it's right, don't change it.

Chapter summary

- Your script is not something to recite by rote. An effective pitch is flexible and adaptable.

- Your script is a platform that will assist your sales team as they engage prospects in meaningful conversations.

- There are two ingredients that go into a successful prospecting call:

  1. Questions that get the prospecting talking early in the conversation
  2. A mindset that regards the call as a discovery call (rather than a sales call).

- Ask questions to uncover (as quickly as possible) the following three things:

  1. Are they a valid prospect?
  2. What is the prospect's current situation?
  3. Where are they in the buying cycle?

- Your script should be in three parts:

  1. Introduction
  2. Questions to build a conversation
  3. Wrap-up.

- A script is meant to read well; it's a spoken pitch, so it's meant to roll off the tongue. Before you finalise it, read your pitch aloud to yourself.

- Time yourself when practicing your pitch. Your introduction shouldn't be any longer than 15 seconds (10-12 seconds is the bullseye).

- Don't neglect qualifying or you'll end up wasting your sales team's time.

- Qualifying questions should be direct, but avoid long strings of questions, which will turn the call (from the prospect's perspective) into an interrogation.

- Online marketing can't qualify prospects. Only P2P prospecting can do that.

- Check in with your salespeople regularly to make sure they haven't radically changed the approach or the pitch. The importance of consistency cannot be overstated.

Step 3

STREAMLINE YOUR PROCESS

W ITHOUT a dedicated process in place, your prospecting efforts are going to be disappointing. Your process consists of *what* you do, *how* you do it, *who* does it, and *when* they do it. The *what* is prospecting, and we've already covered the *how*—you've got your pitch in hand, and you know how to approach (or how to direct your sales team to approach) your prospecting calls. What remains is the *who* and the *when*. Let's look at each of these more closely.

WHO

Your first decision is whether to use your existing sales team, a dedicated prospector or team of prospectors, or, finally, to outsource your prospecting to an expert provider. You don't have to choose only one of these. You can choose one, or two or all three. Some companies use an outsourced solution initially, establishing the metrics and proving the concept, then they take it in-house, using the outsourced provider for overflow work or to ensure that consistency is maintained when a member of the in-house prospecting team leaves the organisation or goes on an extended vacation. Others set up an internal prospecting team, using members of their existing sales team, only to later add a few dedicated prospectors to the team. Still others outsource all of their prospecting and continue to work in partnership with the outsourced firm, freeing up their hands for other key tasks. You may not have to assign prospecting at all. There may be one or two people on your sales team who are eager to do their own prospecting. If so, encourage and reward them. They'll be lifting not only their own sales performance but that of the entire team.

So that you can make an educated choice, let's look at the various options available to you.

Using your existing sales team

Your existing sales team has the most experience selling to your customers, but they might not be the best people for taking on a prospecting role. Salespeople are expensive, and it is usually not a great use of their time to be sitting on the phone calling hundreds of people, day after day. Most salespeople are great at selling face to face. This is, after all, what they do every day. But they might not be as great at generating appointments on the phone. They probably haven't practiced this skill in some time. It also takes a lot of time—time which, in an ideal world, would be better spent talking face to face with interested sales prospects.

Also, because they know your product's features backwards and forwards, sales teams can often end up selling on the prospecting calls, rather than prospecting. It has been drilled into them since they started in sales that they should seize sales opportunities when they arise. If the prospect exhibits any curiosity, salespeople can often go into in-depth discussions, covering the important features at length during what is supposed to be a prospecting call. This is a big mistake (and often a massive time waster). The goal of the call is to gather enough information to determine whether or not an appointment with a sales representative is appropriate. If it is not appropriate or not yet appropriate, a call back is scheduled for another date. Prospecting calls are not an attempt to sell the product. Your existing sales team may find this hard because they are setting an appointment for themselves. The temptation is just too much to resist. They end up spending the majority of their prospecting time answering questions, not asking them.

However, even if they are not telephone prospecting, they can still be prospecting in other ways. Every time they meet someone, whether this is at an event, a networking function, a referral or other contact, or a sales lead from your website, they can use the discovery approach to find out:

1. Whether or not the company is a potential client

2. Who the current decision maker in the organisation is

3. What solution they are currently using

4. What type of prospect they are in terms of account value to your organisation

5. When they are likely to buy.

Even if you're outsourcing some or most of your prospecting, every salesperson should be doing at least some of their own prospecting. It hones their selling skills (helping them uncover needs and issues), and it gives them some accountability. Salespeople who are generating some of their own leads tend to complain less about their leads. Those who are not connected to the prospecting process are the first to complain about the quality of the leads they are being provided. Engage them in the process and these complaints are likely to disappear.

Hiring a dedicated prospector or a prospecting team

This is a good option. By hiring someone to make the prospecting calls, your salespeople can focus on what they do best: meeting qualified prospects and selling to them. That makes a lot of sense. You can hire one prospector or a team of them to look after all of the prospecting required for your sales team. A team ensures continuity; when someone leaves or is promoted, your pipeline won't run dry. This dedicated prospecting team can help you build your database, identify the companies that are good prospects for your company and deliver meeting-ready leads to your sales team.

There are some things to consider before you decide to build your own prospecting team. It is not as straightforward as hiring someone, giving them a phone and a list, and then leaving them to it. Like all salespeople, they need to be brought on board and inducted into the process. They need to be set up, trained, and they need to be managed in an ongoing way if they are going to succeed. Here are some things that can make all the difference when you're setting out on this path. They'll help you make sure that you are well on your way to building a great prospecting team.

1. Hire for the role only

When you hire someone to join your prospecting team, it is important to hire them solely to make prospecting calls. Sometimes companies assign an existing team member who is underutilised. This may be someone who is in a non-sales role and who may not really be all that capable when it comes to making prospecting calls. Where possible, take the time to recruit someone specifically for the role—someone who is keen to make phone calls and to generate qualified sales leads for your sales team.

2. Make the role part time

Making prospecting calls is hard work and, in my experience, there are very few people who can do this full time day after day. So, to start with at least, recruit part-time prospectors. By doing this, you ensure that your prospecting team will stay fresh (burnout is a very real risk for prospectors). When we recruit, we offer our team a 20-hour week, which translates to four hours of calling per day. Keeping their days short means concentrated bursts of prospecting activity. They generate momentum and call it a day well before burnout sets in. In 20 hours of calling, your prospector will make around 350 phone calls and speak with around 100 decision makers. After a year of this, they'll have talked to 5,000 new prospects for your sales team.

3. Give them only one role

Unfortunately, so many companies get this—the biggest challenge of them all—wrong. They hire someone to make prospecting calls and, at some point, they give this person other things to do. Maybe it's an admin role, perhaps it is putting together a sales proposal or doing some research, or it might be supporting the sales team in other ways.

Here's what I call my Golden Rule: If you give someone the job of making prospecting calls, and then also give them another job as well, it doesn't matter what that other job is, it will slowly take over. The volume of prospecting calls they make each day will diminish until there are no calls being made at all. You'll be back at square one.

Whoever you hire to take on this role, make it their only function. Assigning other projects to them shouldn't be an option—make sure that nobody else thinks it's okay to assign them other tasks either.

This means they shouldn't cover for absent salespeople, or others in the company either. Keep their focus solely on prospecting.

4. **Expect them to leave or to ask for a promotion**

   It's only natural for new hires to have aspirations. After as little as a few months, the person you've hired to prospect for you might ask to be promoted. If the promotion is not forthcoming, they might begin to look for a job with another company. Expect and plan for this moment. You can delay it considerably by motivating and managing them well. Make sure that they see themselves (and that they know that you see them) as a key part of the sales team. Some companies deliberately choose to assign an end date to their prospecting roles, telling candidates that, if they make a strong impression in their first year, they'll be offered a full-time position with the sales team. This makes sure that expectations are clear and it keeps the prospector motivated. If anything, their numbers will probably go up as the end of the tenure (and a potential promotion) draws near.

5. **Give them a system and processes, set KPIs**

   Regardless of their role, everybody needs a system to follow and this includes having KPIs. Without these, they'll drift aimlessly because they won't have any idea what prospecting success looks like. Their self-esteem will only be able to handle so much of this aimless drifting. Prospecting is hard work, so your prospectors need support and guidance. They need a script, training, a list and KPIs. They also need motivation, recognition and praise. Be inclusive by making them part of your sales team meetings, and be sure to recognise their contribution towards your sales targets. Leave them sitting alone in a corner of the office, with nobody to talk to and nobody helping them, and they probably won't meet your expectations (let alone surpass them). You'll soon be looking at an empty chair, and you'll have to start the entire process over again.

Setting up an in-house prospecting team is a good option, but companies often underestimate just how much time, effort and ongoing management making this work will require. If you are going to go down this route, it is vital that you take the time to do it right. Spend time developing the prospect list, the script, and the systems you are going to need, and do this *before* you go out and hire a prospector. Don't expect them to come in and tell you how your prospecting campaign should operate, even if they have previous prospecting experience. Set goals for activity (calls and contacts per day) as well as for outcomes (meetings booked). Work closely with them and train them regularly. Perhaps most importantly, make them feel like an integral part of the sales team—because that's what they are.

Outsourcing to a lead generation or sales prospecting company

Outsourcing works extremely well for companies that don't want to deal with the hassle of adding a dedicated prospector (or team of them) to the sales team or with the disruption that invariably comes with assigning prospecting to existing members of the sales team. There are some great business development agencies in Australia and around the world. They will look after the entire process for you, building your prospect database and uncovering great sales leads for your sales team to meet with, filling your pipeline with opportunities and boosting your sales team's performance.

There are four main benefits of outsourcing to a specialist sales prospecting company:

1. They have a team of agents who are already trained and experienced, so you don't have to go through the long process of advertising for, interviewing, recruiting and training a prospector. You also won't have to go through the whole exercise again when they leave and you need to replace them.

2. Prospecting companies have depth, so if someone leaves, they have other agents who can replace them immediately. If you need a second or a third agent to make calls for you (or even an entire team of them), they will be able to scale up (or down) with you.

3. They manage burnout, ensuring that each of their prospectors works on a wide range of projects with an equally wide range of clients. Your pitch never starts to feel tired or uninspired (a definite risk when you've got an in-house prospector who has been working on a single campaign for months on end).

4. Their prospecting agents work in a team environment where everyone is making calls every day. There's virtually no chance that they'll be assigned tasks unrelated to prospecting. They are managed and motivated consistently and by people who know what it takes to bring the best out of their teams.

You may have concerns about hiring people to prospect on your behalf. How, you might ask, will they represent your brand? How will they be able to prospect effectively without knowing all there is to know about your product of service? You may be concerned about the cost. You may be concerned about bringing in a partner who doesn't have a vested interest in your brand.

These are great questions, and you should ask any company that you shortlist for their views on each of them. A good prospecting company has their own reputation to worry about—and that reputation, that brand, is almost certainly founded upon a track record of brand protection and enhancement (not their own brand, but that of their clients). The best way to make sure that your brand is in good hands is to do some research. Find out about other companies they have worked for. Ask them for references and search for good (or bad) reviews online. Testimonials will often tell you whether the company you're considering is one worth partnering with.

When considering your options, also ask about the people who will be making the calls. Who are their agents? What demographic are they from? How long have they been working with the organisation? How does the company select and train its new hires? For instance, the average age of the agents at my company is not, like many other prospecting companies, in the mid-twenties; it is, rather, in the mid-forties. We recruit staff who have the business experience that comes with age, because we know that these professionals can comfortably hold conversations with business decision makers at all levels in all sizes of organisation. This, combined with the variety of campaigns that they work on and a positive work environment, means that our agents stay with us for years. Some have been with us for as long as a decade.

Having industry-specific experience or in-depth knowledge about your product or service might seem important, and these things are important for your salespeople to have, but they're not so important that they are must-haves for those who prospect on your behalf. What *is* important for them to have is experience talking with prospects (particularly those in the size of organisation you want to reach). Remember, they aren't selling your product or service. They are uncovering opportunities. To do this, they need to be able to use a good script to build rapport, to ask good, relevant questions and answer the obvious

FAQs, but their job is not to close the deal. Their job is to take the prospect up to the point where a meeting with one of your salespeople is appropriate—and no further.

Hiring a professional prospecting team to reach out to your target market will definitely cost more than running it yourself in-house. It's easy to imagine that you can hire someone internally for $25 - $30 per hour ($50,000- $60,000 per year on a fulltime basis) but when you factor in the hidden costs of running a prolonged prospecting campaign—training, management, additional resources, and list sourcing just to name a few—you will be looking at double that initial cost and then the extra expense of using a professional team will start to look substantially more palatable.

You've probably heard this all before, and you may be sceptical, so let me show you what I mean.

On top of the hourly rate or salary, you have to add sick leave and holiday pay, wages for public holidays, a commission structure, superannuation, worker's compensation and payroll tax. All of these increase the basic hourly rate by 50%. So you're actually paying $37 - $45 per hour.

Then there are items such as recruitment costs, telephone costs, training, management & ongoing supervision by one of the management team, and other overheads including software licenses, computer and phones. When you factor these in, your initial wage jumps by a further 50% and the real cost of running you own internal sales prospector will come in at somewhere between $50 and $60 per hour.

Add to these costs what happens if you don't hire the right person the first time round, or when your sales prospector leaves for a new role after 9 – 12 months and the amount of time you'll be spending recruiting prospectors and managing their campaigns starts to mount. At this point the scales might start to tip.

It costs us nothing to cut our own grass, trim our own hedges, or clean our own houses, so why do we pay somebody $60 or $70 per hour to do this for us? It's clearly much less expensive to do it ourselves, but our time is worth more to us than the cost of hiring somebody to do the job for us (especially when a professional can do a faster and better job of it than we can). If prospecting is done right, your sales team will be busier than ever meeting with new leads. It's better by far to have their (and your) hands free to do the things that are more important: in the case of your sales team, this is converting qualified prospects into clients.

WHEN

Once you have decided *who* is going to be making the calls, it's time to look at *when*. There is often debate surrounding what time of day and on which days of the week calls should be made. The truth is that, in most cases, it doesn't really matter. There are always people at work throughout the week, and you have just as good a chance of reaching people at 9AM on a Monday as at 4:30PM on a Friday. There are notable exceptions, of course. If your prospects are restaurants, don't call them during the dinner or lunch rushes. If they are retail stores, don't call them around Christmas. But in the main, so long as you're calling during business hours, the time of day and day of the week is not an important factor.

However, you need to consider more than just the prospect. You also need to consider your salespeople. Especially if they've thus far avoided prospecting, they might try to put prospecting off until a more 'convenient' time (a time that never seems to arrive on its own). If you have your sales team making their own prospecting calls, make this their first activity of the day, every day. You might also want to get everyone who is prospecting to do it together. This builds team spirit and a fun sense of competition between your sales staff. Most importantly, it makes the central management role (that is, making sure that it actually gets done) considerably easier.

The next decision you have to make is how many hours per day should be spent on prospecting. It is important to gain momentum in the initial stages, and it's best to assume that it will take longer than you expect to generate qualified sales leads. If you start by assuming that each person making calls will speak to 5 new prospects each hour, and that 1 in 20 prospects will have a qualified need for your services, you can estimate that it will take 1 prospector 4 hours of dedicated calling to generate 1 qualified sales lead (20 prospects @ 5 conversations/hour = 4 hours). Therefore, you'll want your prospectors to be working in four-hour segments throughout the week. This is a half-day's work, which is no small amount, but it's a good place to start. If your prospectors are generating leads much faster, you can always reduce the hours they spend prospecting. Or you can tighten your qualification criteria, which will also slow down the rate that your prospectors are producing qualified leads.

If you hire a dedicated prospector for your team, five prospecting blocks per week should produce steady results. If you're using existing sales resources, you'll probably be making do with less than this. Those in your sales team that you assign prospecting to may not be able to hit the phones every day, but if they're only calling for an hour or two at a time (or less), they'll never gain traction, let alone momentum.

When we start working with a new client, we use these four-hour blocks as a guideline. We allocate 16, 20 or 24 hours of calling per week, usually assigning either one or two agents to each client. We do this because we want our agents to gain traction and produce results quickly. To do so, they need to speak to enough prospects to find several that are ready to meet with our client. If they can't do this after a couple of four-hour blocks, we know that there is an issue that needs to be addressed—usually with either the approach or the script. Our clients expect us to deliver new qualified leads each week (starting in the very first week), and we want to make sure that our approach works for them, so we structure our prospectors' time in such a way that they can be counted upon to produce results.

Using this approach, we are more likely to generate *too many* sales leads than we are to generate too few. If we find ourselves booking more appointments than the sales team can handle, we can always adjust the number of hours we are calling accordingly—reducing our calling, for example, from 24 hours per week to 16 or 20. The same will be true for you too. If your prospecting calls are yielding too many leads, it is simple enough to reduce the number of people or hours that are being spent on prospecting. Adjust the number of prospectors or calling hours until your salespeople are not overwhelmed with new leads but aren't sitting on their hands either.

EVALUATING YOUR PROCESS (METRICS AND KPIs)

Clearly, you will want to know that your prospecting campaign is effective. To evaluate your campaigns you should focus on measuring two things: performance and success. It's not always easy to know when your approach needs to be tweaked slightly or changed entirely. We'll look at that below.

Measuring performance

When you're evaluating your prospecting performance, it's not results you're looking at. Rather, it is activity: how much of it is there, and is it the kind of activity that will produce results (we'll look at the results themselves below). Too often, performance and results are conflated. Think about an Olympic runner. The runner is performing when they are running around the track as fast as their legs will carry them. If they are running (and running quickly) they are performing; their position in relation to the other runners on the track is a measurement not of performance but of success.

You'll want to set performance benchmarks and then make sure that these targets are being met each day or week. The nice thing about performance benchmarks is that you can start measuring them on the first day of a new campaign. There's no wait and see. It's immediate. You should be measuring performance in hours spent calling, calls made per hour or per day, and prospects spoken to per hour or per day.

You should expect your prospectors to make between 15 and 25 phone calls per hour. Not every prospect will be sitting beside their desk waiting for a call from your prospecting team, so many of these calls will not result in a contact. When prospecting in the four-hour blocks I prescribed above, out of the 60 to 100 phone calls they make per prospecting block, you can expect each prospector to speak with between 16 and 28 prospects (4 to 7 each hour).

Measuring success

Once you can see that the activity KPIs are being met, you can turn to measuring success. It will take several months for you to accurately gauge the ultimate success of your prospecting (making sales), which means you need to take a longer-term view of your prospecting campaign. However, you should be able to see the first measurement of success much earlier—this being the number of sales leads your prospectors are producing (per day, per week and per month). I'm often asked how many sales leads (that is, prospects who want to meet now) a client can expect to get, and this is always very difficult to answer. The number produced will depend on how many hours are being spent on prospecting each week. It will also depend on how well your message resonates with your target market, as well as your qualification criteria.

For instance, if prospects in your market are likely to be under a three-year contract with one of your competitors, and you are happy to meet with prospects who have a year or less to run on their contract then statistically speaking, it's likely that two-thirds of your potential prospects are not going to qualify for an immediate meeting. These might be very good future leads, but these leads aren't a measurement of success—not yet at least.

I find that we convert an average of 1 in 18 contacted decision makers into qualified sales leads, but this average sits in the middle of a much broader range. For some of our clients that success rate has been as high as 1 in 3; for others it has been as low as 1 in 50. After a few weeks of prospecting, you'll have an accurate picture of how many hours of prospecting it takes to generate one lead and how many leads you can expect to generate per week.

The final measurement of success is the most obvious one: how many new clients is your prospecting campaign producing, and how quickly is it producing them? Remember that a prospecting campaign is unlikely to accelerate your prospect's buying cycle. If it takes, on average, three to four months to turn a prospect into a sale, telephone prospecting won't change this. You'll need to give prospecting at least six months before you can accurately gauge its success by the number of new clients it has won you. Sure, you should see leads being generated from the first week onwards, and your sales team will be meeting with new prospects from around the second or third week, but if you try to leap to conclusions about the effectiveness of your prospecting before the leads it has fed into your pipeline have had adequate time to work their way through the system, you'll likely be making an important decision prematurely. I've seen far too many companies walk away from prospecting because they were assessing performance on sales results and ROI far too early, only to come back to it six or nine months later because they've realised that they are now gaining new clients from the prospecting they'd done earlier. You need to allow your prospecting activity to run for at least six months as a minimum. Ideally, you should be not assessing overall results until your prospecting campaign has been ongoing for a year.

IS MY STRATEGY WORKING?

One of the most obvious signs that prospecting isn't working is if you are not getting any leads at all. Assuming that the activity (calls made and prospects spoken to) is there, the reason for poor or non-existent results is usually that your approach is not resonating with (or remotely compelling for) your target market. Are your prospectors being cut off before they reach the end of their pitch? This is a symptom with a wide range of causes. It might be that your introduction and pitch aren't resonating with your prospects, or it might be burned out prospectors. It might be a problem with your list, or it might be a problem with the message you're trying to convey, and it's not always easy to tell what's causing the issue.

No matter what the cause, though, if your prospectors aren't making it to the end of their pitch, it's time to start changing your approach. This might mean working with a new crop of prospectors or a new crop of prospects. The first place to make adjustments, though, is your script. As I've highlighted above, it's important to revise and update your script until you find something that works. These changes should be, more often than not, quite small. Tweak your wording or try to cut out super-fluous verbiage. This is the least expensive option, so it's a good place to start. Take it one step at a time. Find out exactly where in the script your prospectors "lose" their prospects. Chances are that something they are saying in the previous sentence or paragraph is turning the prospects off. Change the wording in the problematic section until your prospectors are able to get past this blockage. Keep doing this, paragraph by paragraph if necessary, until your prospectors are getting all the way through the script. If success is still at arm's length, start looking at other possibilities, including how compelling your message is.

Another sign that a change in strategy might be necessary is time wasted in meetings with unqualified prospects. This can usually be addressed by adjusting your qualification criteria. Ask your sales team for feedback on the leads they are seeing (if things are really bad, they'll give it without you having to ask for it). If they report that they're wasting their time meeting with poor prospects, ask them to elaborate. After receiving this feedback, be sure to adjust the qualification criteria accordingly. You can also provide new guidelines for your prospectors, making sure that they are clear about *exactly* what your organisation can and cannot do. If your salespeople are wasting their time meeting with poor prospects, and if there is a common theme (for example, not enough turnover, too few employees, etc.) work a question into your script that will be sure to eliminate these prospects.

If you're not finding success, look at the metrics first (are your prospectors making enough calls? Are enough of these calls resulting in meetings?). If the problem is something else entirely, don't hesitate to go all the way back to the beginning of the process (even as far back as defining your market). If you feel confident that your lists aren't the problem, then it's probably your message or how your prospectors are approaching the calls. Start by taking a closer look at your Prospecting Value Proposition and how it is built into your pitch. The issue might be something as simple as a word or two that is producing a negative reaction, or it might be something larger, like your assumptions about your prospects' issues. Whatever it is, by systematically refining your approach and giving your campaigns enough time to be successful, you'll soon find the right approach.

Chapter summary

- Decide who will be making the calls and when they will be making them. Assign sufficient time to prospecting each week.

- There are three options when it comes to who makes the calls:
  1. Use your existing sales team
  2. Hire a dedicated prospector or build an internal prospecting team
  3. Outsource to a lead generation or sales prospecting company.

- Your salespeople might not be the best resource to draw upon for prospecting. Rather than prospecting, they tend to treat the calls as sales opportunities, which means they answer far more questions than they ask. They end up trying to sell the product, not the meeting.

- Even if they're not prospecting, salespeople should still be encouraged to do some of their own prospecting. This might mean using the discovery process to call a warm lead that's come to them through a digital marketing campaign, or to use it when networking with prospects.

- If you hire a dedicated prospector (or a team of them), be sure to train them and manage them continually. If you don't put a good process in place (and then make sure it stays that way), you will end up wasting time, money, and opportunities.

- When managing your prospectors, keep prospecting sessions short enough to keep energy levels and engagement high, but long enough to gain traction (3-4 hours is good).

- There are four benefits that come with outsourcing to prospecting specialists:

  1. Their experience and expertise
  2. Depth of resources ensures momentum and consistency. There is always a replacement if a team member leaves
  3. Able to minimise burnout by giving staff more variety of projects
  4. No chance of staff being reassigned to unrelated tasks, which means prospecting calls *always* get made.

- The extra costs that come with hiring a firm of prospecting professionals start to look entirely worthwhile when weighed against the resources you'll need to dedicate to managing your prospecting campaigns in house.

- As long as it's during business hours, it doesn't make much of a difference when you or your team make your prospecting calls. Doing them first thing each day tends to ensure that calls don't get put off until a more convenient time.

- Consider having your team make their prospecting calls at the same time. This makes monitoring performance easier, and it builds team spirit and a friendly sense of competition.

- To evaluate your prospecting campaigns measure performance (activity) as well as sales success (results).

- If it becomes clear that you're not getting the desired results, adjust your approach (new pitch, new lists, new prospectors, new processes, etc.), making sure to give each new approach time to work.

Step 4

ALIGN YOUR FOLLOW-UP

THE final step is also the most straightforward. I've spoken in quite a few places about the need for continuity and diligence. Unless you apply this strategy consistently, results will be spotty at best. This is a long-term strategy, and, from the outset, you need to approach it with the future in mind.

Not all of the prospects that your sales team meet with are going to buy from you now. For many, this will be the beginning of a journey. You'll be showing them what you can do for them and how your product or service can make their lives better or easier. The approach to prospects who want to meet today or tomorrow is fairly obvious. Less obvious is the approach to prospects who don't have an immediate need but are still valid prospects. They might need some time to allow their existing solution to prove its worth; they might be under contract for another year or maybe more; they might be looking at a merger or acquisition in the future that will make them an ideal prospect for your organisation. All of these prospects have potential, and you need an aligned process that ensures every single one of them is nurtured and followed up with appropriately.

Depending on the status of the prospect (for example, whether they have met with a representative from your company or just been called by one of your prospecting team), you'll decide who will be assigned the follow-up. It might be the prospecting team, or it might be a member of your sales team. Ideally, once a relationship has been established, the same person who talked to or met with the prospect at last contact should be the one responsible for the follow-up call.

Your marketing team can look after the marketing material, sending relevant information to each prospect. This material should endeavour to educate and persuade the prospect, and, if possible, it should reference their current problems and how you can solve them. How we nurture prospects determines whether we have their trust or not. Get this right and you'll be in pole position when the flag drops. When they decide to purchase, it's your company that will leap to mind.

Marketing materials are good, but they should always complement, rather than replace, your sales team's regular follow-up phone calls. These calls might only take a minute or two—just enough to check in and confirm that nothing has changed with the prospect since the last contact. Whether stated outright or not, these calls tell the prospect that you are eager to win their business and that you will be there for them the moment they are ready to buy.

I'm often asked how follow-up should be structured, particularly how often the sales team should be contacting prospects who don't have an immediate need. The appropriate length of time between contacts will vary depending on your industry and the length of the buying cycle, but, more importantly, it depends on what the prospect says during the previous call. A prospect who is under contract for two more years probably needs a call no more than once a year. If you've developed any kind of rapport with the prospect, it might be appropriate to double this, contacting them every six months. These follow-up calls should build upon the existing rapport to further increase your company's profile. Some prospects will say that they will have or may have a need in the future. Ask them when a call back is appropriate, and then make sure you follow up when you said you would.

If you forget to make these follow-up calls, you won't be doing yourself any favours. When the prospect is ready to purchase, it's unlikely they'll remember the conversation with you or your sales team. They will go online and choose one of the suppliers they find out there. It might be you, but why leave that to chance when a few quick follow-up calls can cement your relationship with them so that they choose to buy from you instead of searching online. For those prospects who leave the door open to future business with you, a good rule of thumb is to contact them by phone every six months.

It's important that, when you call, you have an ostensible reason for the call. You need to have something to say, something to discuss. Just calling the prospect and asking if they're ready to buy yet will probably meet the same kind of response as the pushy sales calls I've talked about earlier in this book. This doesn't mean that the call should only be a friendly conversation. Idle chitchat can build relationships, sure, but it won't move you much closer to an appointment or a sale. Prepare for follow-up calls by writing a short description of something your company has done or changed since you and the prospect last spoke. Barring this, let them know about the next marketing email that they are about to receive and highlight something in that email (a recent case study or testimonial) that you think they will find interesting. Calls like this can make Marketing's email blasts far more effective. Mention something briefly that is explored in more depth in an email from Marketing and you'll increase readership. It's one hand working with the other.

Some companies assign follow up to Marketing. That's fine if your sales team and your marketing department are sharing the prospecting load, but Marketing definitely shouldn't be the only department in charge of follow-up. Having Marketing manage the follow-up process is better than nothing, but I've yet to encounter a company that has made this work as well as when both Sales and Marketing are nurturing.

The worst thing you can do is allow your sales team to stop making follow-up calls entirely, even for a limited time. The moment you stop making follow-up calls is the same moment that you effectively begin to undo all the prospecting and sales work you've done up to that point.

Following up also ensures that you are maintaining the accuracy of your database. People change jobs every two or three years, so within a year one-third of your prospects may have moved on. If you're calling regularly, you may be the first one to build a relationship with the new decision maker. Regular and structured follow-up keeps you front of mind with your prospects, makes sure your marketing materials are read and that will keep the sales rolling in through your front door, week after week.

In the following pages is how the prospecting timeline looks when we work with our clients. Your prospecting programme will probably follow a similar structure.

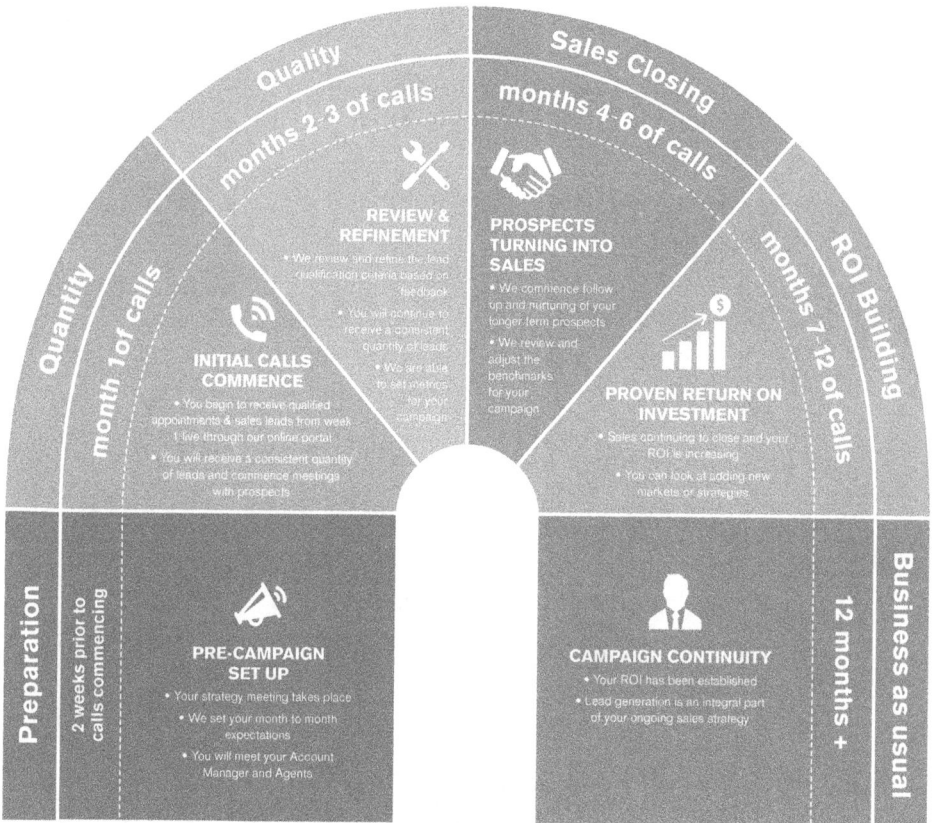

PRE-CAMPAIGN SET UP

- Initial Strategy meeting takes place where you meet your Account Manager and Agents. It is from this meeting that your campaign is set up
- The strategy / approach for your campaign is determined and scripts, FAQs, email templates and other background information is developed
- Your meeting calendar is set up as is the client portal for dynamic online reporting
- Prior to calls commencing a training session is held with your Account Manager and Agents ensuring campaign objectives are clear; there is a complete understanding of your product or service and company and any possible objections are addressed.

We take the time to set up your campaign properly from the start to ensure we deliver you remarkable results.

INITIAL CALLS COMMENCE

- The focus of this month is on developing a consistent volume of leads
- Initial calls commence and you will begin to receive qualified appointments and sales leads from the first week
- You will be notified of leads via email and through our online client portal
- Your feedback on appointments begins via our client portal, this is critical to assist in refining approach if needed to optimise the campaign

By the end of the first month you will be attending meetings with prospects.

REVIEW & REFINEMENT

- Your campaign will continue to deliver a consistent number of sales leads
- Refine the lead qualification criteria based on appointment feedback, ensuring only high quality leads are provided
- With some experience we are now able to put in place campaign metrics and benchmarks
- Consistent number of meetings with qualified prospects will continue
- You may also be attending second meetings with qualified prospects from the earlier months
- Sales proposals are being issued and followed up

You will be seeing a sales pipeline developing and an early indication of likely sales.

PROSPECTS TURNING INTO SALES

- Lead generation continues in line with the developed campaign metrics
- Ongoing refinement of the campaign and lead qualification criteria
- Begin leading nurturing and follow-up calls to longer term opportunities
- Sales opportunities begin to close and you will start to see a return on investment

At this stage we can start looking at approaching new markets or territories as well as possibly scaling up your campaign.

PROVEN RETURN ON INVESTMENT

- Lead generation continues with ongoing monitoring
- A consistent volume of leads are now converting to prospects and customers
- Some of the nurtured prospects from earlier months are now also turning into qualified sales leads

More prospects are turning into customers with the campaign ROI continuing to build.

CAMPAIGN CONTINUITY

- ROI is established and proven
- Lead generation is now an integral part of your ongoing sales strategy
- More sales are converting from sales prospects you met with earlier in the campaign.

Most clients continue with lead generation as a long term strategy with consistent results ongoing.

Chapter summary

- Prospecting is a long-term strategy and needs to be approached with the future in mind.

- Continuity and diligence are crucial to prospecting success, so it's important to ensure that you're following up with your prospects.

- Whoever made last contact with the prospect should be the one who is responsible for the follow-up call. This gives the relationship a sense of continuity.

- Marketing materials are a good way to nurture prospects, but they should complement rather than take the place of follow-up calls.

- If a prospect leaves the door open to doing business with you in the future, a good rule of thumb is to contact them every six months or so.

- When following up, be sure to have something to discuss (ideally, some recent development or a glowing testimonial).

- Sales and Marketing should share the nurturing load.

- Without an aligned follow-up process, the majority of the work that went into your prospecting campaign will be wasted.

CONCLUSION

You now have everything you need to fill your pipeline with qualified prospects, to start two-way conversations with them, and to convert these new prospects into customers. You've started with the understanding that there is more out there for your company—that there is a gigantic and unexplored part of your market just below the waterline. You've learned how to look below the waterline and identify this untapped market. You've also learned how to build a database of suitable prospects with the help of a list broker. And finally you've learned how to define your Prospecting Value Proposition, refine your pitch, streamline your process, and align your follow-up.

Doing one, or two, or three of these things won't make much of a difference to your bottom line. Without a good list to prospect with, my four-step process won't be very successful. Without defining your Prospecting Value Proposition, you won't be able to craft a winning script. Without putting the correct, robust process in place, today's results will be, at best, inconsistent and your sales team won't have much to follow up with down the track. Each part of the process reinforces each of the others.

Remember, as well, that there's a secret ingredient: consistency. If you don't add consistency to the recipe, results will fall significantly short of their potential. Stay the course and refine your approach, honing your script and your Prospecting Value Proposition, and you'll soon be enjoying explosive sales growth. P2P prospecting done the right way is a business multiplier. It turns potential results into actual ones.

Let's look at an example. Say that customers in your market are likely to come off contract or change suppliers three years after they have bought your competitor's product. Let's also say that you have 3,000 *qualified* prospects in your database, with each one being a known opportunity. As each year contains 260 business days, over 3 years, that's a total of 780 business days in the next three years, over which these 3,000 contacts will be coming off contract. That means your sales team will have 3.8 prospects to sell to every day for the next 3 years. That's 19 new sales opportunities each week. If you sell to just 10% of these qualified prospects, that's 2 new clients each week. If you sell to 30% of these prospects, that's 6 new clients each week. And if you sell to 50% of them it's 9 new clients each week. What would 9 new clients each week mean for your business?

Success like this will come as a result of your newfound ability to intersect the customer while they are still in the earliest stages of their buyer's journey. A recent study conducted by Duke University researchers looked at the browsing history of 1,000 customers who had bought digital cameras online. What they found was that these customers had researched digital cameras online an average of 6 times over the 15 days preceding their purchase. They were comparing different models, looking at customer reviews, etc. Here's what was most interesting about the study: the majority of those surveyed purchased the camera they researched first. Their research was mostly about confirming their first choice—not about making their choice (it had, in effect, already been made).

Now apply this to your customers. If they already know you when they start researching suppliers, they will be more likely to purchase from you. They know that you want their business, and if your marketing materials and salespeople are worth their salt, they'll have an extremely favourable view of your company and your product or service. You're starting the race in pole position. If your close rate is 10% or 20% at the moment, the right prospecting programme, by putting you in pole position when most of your races begin, could double or even triple your closing rate. As you'll have seen by now, P2P prospecting isn't just about talking to more people; it's about combining a structured dialogue with a personal approach that boosts your chances of winning new clients, and then applying that approach every day, every week, every month, and every year.

You'll also be converting dormant accounts to active ones and turning new prospects into new customers. You'll be adding contacts into your database (just as you always have) from networking events, tradeshows, referrals, online enquiries, and so on, and you'll be nurturing and talking to these new prospects in ways that are significantly more likely to result in winning their business. Your sales team will become better at selling, and your marketing team will start seeing much better open and click through rates (all thanks to the conversations your prospectors are having with prospects). This will turn long-term prospects (who used to be largely ignored except by Marketing) into warm and hot leads. This is the power of P2P prospecting and the discovery conversation.

You'll be making your database a more powerful marketing and sales tool with each contact you make, filling it with relevant information about the prospect's preferences and about the company's particular issues. You'll have the right contact info, and the decision makers will know your salespeople (often by name). You'll be chipping away at your iceberg, shaping it with powerful tools, but you'll also be adding to it by using the right search criteria to uncover new prospects. You'll know more about these prospects than your competitors. You'll know what they need, and you'll know how to first market to them and then sell to them. Your marketing team will be able to target subsets of your database with persuasive messages and relevant content. Your prospects will see you as a thought leader and a potential partner. You'll be the provider of choice.

As I have said, this won't come easy—if it was easy, everyone would be doing it. You'll have to work hard, and you'll have to do it consistently. Your sales team will have to pick up the phone every single day to talk to new prospects and nurturing existing ones. They'll turn into better information gatherers, and this information will power your sales process. The approach I've outlined in this book is simple, but it becomes easier the more dedication and consistency you apply to it—you need that much to do even the simplest things in life well. But this is where most people fail and why so many people have declared that telephone prospecting is dead, preferring the easier route of online advertising and e-nurturing. Twenty-first-century digital marketing techniques, once spectacularly successful, are now subject to diminishing returns. Marketers and salespeople are scrambling, looking for the next great sales and marketing tool to come along. All the while, the answer is right under their noses. Those of us who know what works are quite content to use a powerful method that is all the more effective because so few people are using it.

Make the choice to make P2P telephone prospecting an essential part of your sales strategy. Start small, start slowly, and build momentum as you go. Start with a list of 1,000 companies (your iceberg might be much, much larger than this, but a list of 1,000 companies is a good place to start). When you've contacted all of them and fed the qualified prospects into your pipeline, add another 1,000. Repeat. It's this simple. In time, you'll understand the contours of your *entire* iceberg. This might take a year; it might take even longer than that if your market is very large, but along the way you'll be selling, and you'll be the star of your organisation.

Today, as I write this book, the economy is relatively strong. In some industries it has recovered to (or even surpassed) pre-2008 levels. It's a feast out there right now for those with a savvy sales strategy. If, for any reason, rough winds and choppy seas return, having a first-rate sales strategy in place will put you in a strong position to weather the storm. With a full pipeline, you'll still be growing, even in a recession. Do people stop buying in tough times? No they don't. They are, though, more careful about what they purchase and, more importantly, from whom they purchase.

The strategies I've discussed in this book are designed to build relationships, and it's these relationships that determine how money is spent—especially when money is tight. Get out there today. Dip below the waterline and start introducing yourself to your market. Today's prospects will be tomorrow's customers.

Good luck!

ABOUT THE AUTHOR

Richard Forrest is the Founder and Managing Director of Forrest Marketing Group, one of Australia's top B2B sales prospecting companies. Richard has spent almost 30 years in the world of sales, sales management and sales training and has built and managed teams of sales people across the world, teaching them how to sell successfully.

Richard started Forrest Marketing Group in 2006 to provide high quality B2B sales prospecting and lead generation solutions to businesses struggling to find enough qualified leads for their sales teams. Now, with a team of almost 80 staff in their offices on Sydney's Northern Beaches, as well as a sister company in the UK, Richard works with some of the biggest brands in Australia, and Forrest Marketing Group is recognised as an industry pioneer and leader. Since 2006, they have made more than 4,000,000 phone calls for over 1,500 organisations. These calls have generated more than 150,000 appointments that have turned into hundreds of millions of dollars in sales.

Richard is passionate about the power of P2P prospecting and demonstrating how a great conversation delivered over the phone is an integral part of the sales process. He wants to show companies how to take back complete control of their sales funnel and address their entire market rather than only a fraction of it.

For more information about Richard, please visit:

www.richardforrest.com.au

WHERE TO GO FROM HERE

To take the first steps to setting up a sales prospecting team (either internally or outsourced), the first thing you should do is download the free P2P Prospecting Brief, which can be found at **www.fmgroup.com.au** under Resources to help you to work through your prospecting strategy.

If you would prefer to discuss your needs one on one, please call Richard in Sydney on +61 2 9939 6888.